Finding Myself Inside: When a Prison Sentence Becomes God's Gift of Love

Niven A Neyland

Finding Myself Inside: When a Prison Sentence Becomes God's Gift of Love Copyright © by Niven A Neyland. All Rights Reserved.

Names of inmates and some others have been changed to protect privacy

Contents

Foreword *v*

1. Introduction *1*
2. The Collision *5*
3. Early Days *13*
4. A Second Taste *20*
5. Working And Drinking *27*
6. Change Through Decision *36*
7. Relapse *41*
8. Relationships *47*
9. No Time to Mourn *56*
10. A Show Of Force *63*
11. County Court And The Astute Judge *69*
12. The Dawning: Pentridge Prison *77*
13. The Realisation *84*
14. Visits *91*
15. The Missing Kettle *98*
16. Room With a View *105*
17. Church Comes to Prison *111*
18. Had Enough, Time for Change! *119*
19. Living in the Here and Now *128*
20. In God's Hands *136*
21. Planting and Watering *144*
22. Unusual Characters *150*

23. Change and Christmas *158*
24. The Reaping *163*
25. Plom's Disease *170*
26. More Unique People *179*
27. Anger Management *186*
28. Free At Last! *193*
29. Finding a New Normal *200*
30. Prison Ministry *207*
31. Forgiveness Heals *214*
32. Epilogue: Final Reflections *223*

Appendix 1: Helps For Getting Through Life and Prison *233*
Appendix 2: A Prayer for a Relationship with God *236*
Appendix 3: Bible Personages Familiar With Prison *239*

Foreword

Niven Neyland has written his compelling story, and I can honestly say there are few other stories that are quite as honest, insightful and hopeful as this one. To live with the horror and shame of being responsible for the death of one's own brother, and to accept that responsibility and allow it to work for good in his own life, and in the lives of many others is remarkable.

I have visited in a few of the prisons in our State – and always found it a chilling experience. But I have never read or understood what it is like as a day to day experience for those locked inside. This story charts that experience so well. The daily routine, the anxiety, the shame, the anger and the longings are all here in raw detail. But in the midst there are also insights into lessons learned about human frailty, and the power of forgiveness. If there is ever a place that needs the out workings of the gospel it is our prisons. Niv Neyland's story exemplifies this magnificently.

I thought again of those powerful words of our Lord's in Matthew 25. "For I was hungry, and you gave Me something to eat; I was thirsty, and you gave Me a drink; I was a stranger, and you invited Me in; naked, and you clothed Me; I was sick, and you visited Me; I was in prison, and you came to Me". The righteous will answer and ask me when? And the King will answer '…to the extent that you did it to one of these brothers of Mine, even the least of them, you did it to Me." The work of ministry in prisons is indeed holy ground; as is ministry in hospitals, refugee support, and soup kitchens. In the 'least of them' there is the image of God. I think we see this beautifully expressed in the transformative work of God in and through Niv Neyland.

In his own words:

Had I not gone to prison, I would likely have spent the last thirty years building a successful business and living for myself with God coming second, just as I had so many times in the past. My sentence put a stop to that. I was taken to a dark place where God Himself was my light, and the course of my life changed.

What a powerful testimony! May God continue to protect and use you mightily Niv in the calling he has placed on your life.

I also pay tribute to the faithfulness of his wife Heather; her love, forbearance and grace is very evident. I am sure that her story is worthy of a book also. There is so much to be said for the need for that 'outside' community of hope, forgiveness and love in the role of visiting prisoners and walking with them once they come out.

I am honoured to be a Patron of two organisations with which Niven has had significant involvement. *Prison*

Fellowship, who visit prisoners, run rehabilitative programs and care for families of offenders, and *Friends of Dismas*, the church assisting adults on parole, ex-prisoners, and their family and friends, to grow in Christian faith. It is my prayer that these ministries can continue their good work and that many more Christians and churches capture the vision for supporting prison ministry, both inside the walls and with those who have been released.

Rev Tim Costello AO
Executive Director of Micah Australia
Senior Fellow for the Centre for Public Christianity
Melbourne, Australia
January 2021

1

Introduction

Not everyone finds it easy to venture into the past. It can be embarrassing to open the closet and bring out the skeletons. At my current age, I could likely hide much of my past life, leaving it buried in the files of history. But in doing so, I would end up whitewashing myself to the point of becoming irrelevant to others who struggle. Honest "warts and all" personal stories can be powerful tools for helping others. So it is in that context I've chosen to dig my own past out of its burial plot and share it with you in these pages.

In brief, I was involved many years ago in an alcohol-related vehicle collision. This event occurred on my birthday, and in the process, I lost my only brother. While there were mitigating circumstances, it was ultimately my fault. Birthdays have never been the same since the collision, but life goes on—and on.

I haven't had a drink since that day. Besides the terrible tragedy of losing my brother, I ended up on a roller-coaster ride of injustice and duplicity that ultimately resulted in losing my business, followed by being sentenced to prison for alcohol-related manslaughter, leaving my young pregnant wife on her own.

I'm guessing there isn't a single person who hasn't struggled with some form of "inner demon," whether alcohol or drug addiction, sexual immorality, financial temptations, etc. Many overcome their demons and go on to live successful lives. Others end up in prison or lose families, friends, jobs, and money. Some even go to early graves with that demon still driving them. Some struggles are obvious to others while other struggles remain hidden behind closed doors.

"Life is a struggle" is a common saying, the implication being that life is supposed to be a struggle because the struggle is what makes us stronger. But if the "inner demon" a person is struggling with is more powerful than the struggler, then that struggle isn't making the person stronger but just pulling them under. To put it another way, if a swimmer is caught in a fast current too powerful to swim against, the swimmer has only limited control and ends up being swept along by the current no matter how much they might struggle.

Typical critical comments when we see others caught in such an undertow include: "Well, she shouldn't have tried those drugs. She got what she deserved . . . If he wasn't drinking, he wouldn't be in this mess . . . If you play with fire, you get burnt. It's his own fault!"

But people get sucked into the wrong things for a variety of reasons, often not realising there is a trap awaiting them up ahead. It's easy to throw out the platitude that winning any struggle is just one good decision away. The truth is that many people find it hard to make that one vital choice and commit to it. They simply can't muster up the resolve and end up losing hope.

That was once me. When I think of those days and my struggle with sin, especially alcohol, I can't help but remember a 1980s gospel song entitled *Mercy Re-Wrote my Life*. The lyrics basically sum up the depths of God's mercy and the great lengths to which He is prepared to go in order to turn our lives around for His glory. He knows what it will take to get us to stand up and take notice. Unfortunately for us, this often means He has to allow us to go through some serious hurt and grief, whether financial, social, or as in my case, physical and emotional, for us to get the message and turn to Him unconditionally.

Looking back now, I can see many times when God tried to reach me but I wouldn't surrender. I just kept living my own way by my own rules, and eventually God's patience ran out.

I believe in the sovereignty of God as taught in the Bible. I also believe God has His hand on every situation in a Christian's life, even turning our foolishness around for His glory. From this perspective, I share with you a brief narrative of my own journey. One that took me to prison and out the other side. During this journey, I had no doubt whatsoever that God had His divine hand on me, and I felt blessed beyond measure. I learned to be free while inside the walls of a prison, and only God can do that.

My hope and prayer is that you will be blessed and even personally helped by my story, "warts and all." Whatever struggles you may be going through in your own life, I pray that you will experience God's presence just as I experienced God's presence throughout this unusual saga.

2

The Collision

June 5th, 1990, was my thirty-fifth birthday. Trade was a bit slow at the garden supplies store in Sydenham, Victoria. A suburb about twenty kilometres northwest of Melbourne where my brother and business partner John and I sold soil, used railway sleepers, and various other garden products.

The phone rang. It was a friend who worked close by at the famous Calder Park Thunderdome. The project was former Australian car-racing champion Bob Jane's bid at bringing the USA NASCAR race to Australia. My brother John and I had bought tickets for the inaugural race celebrations in 1988, the first time a NASCAR race had been held outside the United States. Many top American drivers had come to Australia to compete. It was an exhilarating race, and John and I had great seats.

Knowing it was my birthday, my friend had called to invite me to join him and another mutual friend for a counter lunch at the Diggers Rest Hotel a few kilometres away. We hadn't caught up for some time, and the thought of a good lunch and a few laughs sounded appealing. As lunchtime approached, I jumped in the Audi to leave. On the spur of the moment, I opened the car window and invited my brother John to come with me. With the day's slow traffic, our employees could look after the place while we were gone. John got in, and away we drove.

I had other reasons to celebrate that day besides my birthday. Eight months earlier, I'd met the most incredible young woman, Heather Milne. About eleven years younger than me, she was beautiful with her blond hair and gentle blue-green eyes. I'd grown to love her relaxed nature, easy laugh, and above all, her godly Christian character. I'd proposed to her almost four months earlier on Valentine's Day, and she'd said yes. We were getting married in just seven weeks, and John was going to be my best man.

At the hotel, we met our friends, ordered our meals, then ate with plenty of jokes and laughter over old times. We'd known the family of one of them for more than twenty years. I'd played football with him, gone on surfing trips and other holidays when we were younger, and knocked around the streets with him in our teen years. We were good mates and still are today.

As we ate lunch, we played some pool and had some drinks. We lingered on into the afternoon, enjoying a few more drinks, some bags of chips, and a few more games of pool. It was good to catch up with friends. But my greatest pleasure was seeing John happy and enjoying the afternoon. He'd recently gone through bitter divorce proceedings that followed a three-year marriage separation, all of which had taken a heavy toll on him.

When we finally left the hotel, I got behind the wheel. When John and I went out together, I always seemed to be the one driving while he relaxed. We were travelling along the Calder Highway, approaching the right turn we'd have to make at Calder Park Drive just past the raceway.

Crossing that section of highway was precarious at the best of times. No one liked being caught stationary at that turnoff for fear of being side-swiped or rear-ended. But these last few weeks it was even worse as the Victoria department of transport was doing all kinds of road construction. This had led to orange safety bunting strung everywhere, making our side of the road very narrow. Cars turning right, as I was about to do, needed to hug the white line and pick a gap in the oncoming traffic.

Shifting down through the gears, I picked my gap and whipped across the highway as I'd done countless times in numerous cars and trucks returning from product deliveries and social outings. But this time my calculations were faulty, taking me directly into the path of a looming car travelling at a hundred kilometres an hour. I hadn't even seen the vehicle approaching before it slammed into us, flipping the Audi over. We landed on our roof and came to an abrupt halt on the roadside.

I hung upside-down, suspended by my seatbelt, as people began milling around the Audi. I moved my fingers and toes to see if anything was broken, then cautiously turned my head from side to side. All seemed okay.

Thank goodness! I thought, then turned my head far enough

to see my brother. John was also suspended upside-down in his seatbelt, but I could see bloody air bubbles coming out of his nostrils. I would later learn that he'd taken the full impact of the collision on the left side of his skull. A few seconds later, though it seemed a lifetime, the bubbles ceased. My housemate, business partner, mate, and older brother who'd protected me from time to time as older brothers do was gone forever. All I could do in the deafening silence of that car cabin was just look at him.

The fact that John was actually dead came crashing down on me in that moment. A few seconds later, I finally got my act together and crawled out of the wreck. The fire brigade was already on the scene. Thankfully, one of them was a mate of mine who stepped forward to stop me before I could rush around to John's side of the car. "Don't go around there, Niv!"

Ignoring his comment, I tried to side-step him. He again moved across my path. "Niv, you don't want to go around there!"

I obeyed his second warning. I could now see the car that had hit me. It was in bad shape as was the driver. Traffic was backing up in both directions. The ambulance and police soon arrived. Due to that leisurely lunch, they quickly discovered alcohol on my breath.

This resulted in a mixture of insinuations. The police accused me of "swerving all over the road" on the way down the highway, "slurring my speech," and being "wobbly on my feet" at the scene. Thankfully, the ambulance personnel with whom I'd spent most of my time at the scene stated in their report that I was "lucid and coherent" at all times.

After the initial questioning from police and checks from the onsite ambulance team, I was taken to a hospital for a further check-up and blood tests. Then I performed the hardest task I've ever undertaken. I rang my mother to tell her I'd just killed her only other son. Mum thought I was joking as I had a reputation for practical jokes. Nothing could have prepared her for the overwhelming truth of my phone call.

Experts say that losing a child is one of the most agonising experiences on this earth since parents have every expectation their children will outlive them, not the other way around. I had just put Mum through that agony. The conversation shot me back to when my dad died many years before. I was seventeen and had just visited him in the Intensive Care Unit (ICU) at the Royal Melbourne Hospital.

He was only sixty-five years old and had seemed fine after a minor operation when I'd visited him the previous evening. But within twenty-four hours, his health had deteriorated to the point that they'd moved him from a ward to ICU. Lying on his side drugged to the hilt with his eyes still closed, he'd asked, "Is that you, Niv?"

"Yes, it's me!" I responded.

He fell asleep and to my knowledge didn't open his eyes again in this life. When I got home from the hospital later that night, I found Mum and one of my sisters, Helene, crying bitterly. During my drive home, the hospital had rung with the unexpected news. Dad had been chronically ill, but he'd always come back to us, so his sudden passing was a bewildering shock.

The pain of that moment and my mum's tear-streaked face came rushing back to me as I explained to Mum about John. After informing Mum, I rang each of my four sisters. They too thought at first that I was joking. I experienced the same comments, reactions, and emotions as I had from Mum, but thanks to God, no hostility. We were all just trying to come to terms with our loss.

Our employees back at the garden supplies store had seen a report of the accident on the news. When John and I never returned to work, they put two-and-two together and guessed we must have been involved. The next day I kept the business closed, though we did reopen the following day.

The day after the collision, I notified my brother's ex-wife about his death and funeral, which proved a major mistake. Though they'd been separated for almost three years, the divorce papers hadn't been finalized at the time of John's death. She'd had no part in our business since the separation, and the profits were virtually non-existent due to a recession the country was going through. But she saw the business as a money tree and immediately came after me for what she claimed as John's and her two-thirds of the business.

During the following months between the collision and my court case, the oddest, coldest sense of responsibility hit me, and I operated as a very different person. No tears, just a big job to do. I couldn't cry about John. I don't know what it was, but I recall clearly one night after work standing in the shower—his shower in his house since I'd been living with him at the time of the collision—and thinking I should have shed a tear or been crying at some stage.

I didn't even shed a tear at his funeral, which for me was a walk of shame far worse than prison would be. The funeral parlour was packed. I stood there in front of all those people like a guilty murderer in front of a room full of judges. John and I were both members of the local volunteer fire brigade, and they'd made a guard of honour for John as the casket was carried out between them. Many mourners came up to reassure me, "It's not your fault! It could have happened to anyone."

Of course at that stage, they didn't know the full story. Seven weeks later, I married my sweetheart as planned, though our big day was touched with sadness over the absence of my best man and brother. For thirteen months after the crash, I continued our business until the day I was thrown off the property through the machinations of John's ex-wife.

During those months, I hoped and prayed and believed that the court case pending against me for culpable driving under the influence would be dismissed without jail time. Losing my only brother had been a painful enough punishment. The last thing I wanted was to abandon my new bride while I served a prison sentence.

But just five weeks after my former sister-in-law had me forcibly removed from the business John and I had worked so hard to build, I found myself in prison, leaving my beautiful young wife in the desperate situation of being alone, out of work, three months pregnant, and with her immediate family five hundred kilometres away.

For the fourteen months that had passed from the collision to being escorted through the gates of Her Majesty's Pentridge Prison in Coburg, Victoria, shame had been my constant shadow. And now that shame had caught up to me.

3

Early Days

I was born a blond-haired, blue-eyed child in the Royal Women's Hospital, Melbourne, Victoria, to Niven and Beryl Grace Neyland. Dad was Niven Neyland II, his own father Niven Neyland I, and I was the third. Granddad Neyland signed up for the Boer War in South Africa with his own dad. Not long after returning to Australia, he married my grandmother, Linda May Pryse, and had four children, including my dad, before signing up for WWI. After that war, he fathered one more child before passing away ten years later, leaving Grandma to raise the kids alone.

Many years later, Grandma moved to the rural community of Sydenham, Victoria. My dad met my mum in the nearby city of Ballarat. They had six children, four girls—Lael, Carmel, Beth, and Helene—followed by John, then me three-and-a-half years later. Dad suffered from chronic asthma in days when asthmatics had little preventative medicine. This made earning a good living difficult, so we were very poor. Among the livelihoods my parents tried were poultry farming and egg production.

Initially, we lived in caravans on Grandma's war pension

property, so some locals used to call us gypsies. While I was too young to worry about that stigma, my mum and older sisters carried the burden of indignity. Eventually, my parents built a cottage in the middle of a paddock on Grandma's property. Made from used bricks with cement render on the outside, it had very pretty second-hand stained-glass windows and a tin roof. Others might not have thought much of it, but to my folks it was a palace.

A few hundred metres toward the rear of the property was a hole in the ground once used as a garbage dump where we kids liked to forage around. One day my older brother John found a dirty old teddy bear there and gave it to me. Another local kid, Jimmy, grabbed it from me and began running home. Jimmy had seven brothers and sisters, and the family was even poorer than we were. But principle is principle, and John chased him down, rescuing my bear. Mum wanted to throw it out, but after much pleading from me, she washed it, and I had it for years.

Sydenham has a dry, barren climate with rocky soil, so few wanted to live there. Its main products during my growing-up years were wheat and other grains along with sheep and cattle grazing. When the rains did come, a torrent swept down past Grandma's property to a small creek where John and I often caught frogs. We would play in the muddy deluge to our hearts' content, dropping leaf boats into the surging waters as we pretended we were famous international boat racers.

An old railway sleeper across the narrow creek allowed us

to take a shortcut to school. We'd climb over a dry-stone wall past a huge old cactus before crossing the main road to get to the school. John and I would pause to swordfight the spiky cactus leaves with pretend swords made of old sticks. We always kept a sharp lookout for snakes, which seemed to be everywhere when we were kids. I was around ten years old when I killed my first snake as it reared to bite me.

Though we were financially poor, we were far from spiritually or emotionally poor. My parents ensured that an atmosphere of love and godliness enveloped our home. Mum was raised in the church from a child and was a committed Christian when she met Dad, as were her parents. Dad was not raised a Christian, but from the first time he'd read the Bible, he'd known Jesus Christ was real, and he gave his heart to Jesus Christ before he met Mum.

One job Dad could do despite his ill health was driving a taxi. This provided opportunities to speak to many people about Jesus. Dad had a natural way of chatting that got people thinking about eternity and where they would end up after death. When his asthma kept him housebound, he used the time to read and study the Bible. This led to hosting church meetings in our home. My earliest memories include walking between the feet of the adults as they gathered for Bible studies and prayer and praise meetings around an old foot-pump reed organ. My four older sisters all gave their hearts to Jesus and became born-again Christians. John and I followed much later.

Mum used to joke that Dad was constantly bringing home

stray people in need of a meal or company even when she didn't have enough food for our own family. When the money jar was completely empty, Mum would send one of the girls down to the local store for "half a pound of broken biscuits, please," so as to have something to feed company. Still, she always managed to put food on the table.

We lived on my grandmother's property in Sydenham until the end of my second year of primary school, when my parents bought a truck-stop called *The Boomerang Cafe* in the town of Keilor just a few kilometres towards Melbourne from Sydenham. The truck-stop was open about eighteen hours a day, seven days a week, as trucks and other vehicles heading to and from Melbourne stopped there night and day while locals came in to shop as well. All of us kids along with my parents had jobs in the business.

John and I were ten and seven when we started working at the truck-stop. Our main job was to get up at six o'clock in the morning and bring in crates of milk bottles, neatly stacking the bottles in the café's two fridges. This included rearranging any leftover milk from the day before and moving it to the front for quick sale. As brothers, we'd have contests to see who was quickest at stocking the fridge without breaking bottles, kneeling down beside our respective fridge doors like racing drivers waiting for the starter's gun. We'd set clocks sitting on top of the fridges to record our daily contest times.

"Ready, set, go!" one of us would yell to start the race. The first to finish would yell "finished!" Then we'd see how long it took for the other to finish. Sometimes one of us would cheat, yelling "finished" while still moving the final bottle from its cradle.

"No, that didn't count! You cheated!" the other one would yell out.

When finished, we'd place the wire crates out at the front of the shop for recycling empty bottles. Then we'd get ready and head to school a short walk away. The living quarters at the rear of the truck-stop were small and overcrowded with a family of eight, making us feel as though the word "poor" was still written on our foreheads. But Keilor had a nice village atmosphere, and living at the truck-stop helped us kids quickly get to know lots of locals and make friends.

It was during this time that I got my first taste of alcohol. I was about ten years old and visiting at a friend's house when his father asked me to open a bottle of beer for him. I cheekily took a mouthful before bringing it to him. Even today I recall the taste, the bubbles up my nose, and the euphoric feeling it gave my young mind. To a ten-year-old, it felt fantastic even if for a moment.

I didn't realise then that just one sip would eventually become the catalyst for my downhill slide. I hadn't been brought up to drink alcohol. Dad and Mum had higher spiritual goals for me, and even at that young age, I knew I'd been called to a spiritual purpose. But as Jesus said in Matthew 26:41: "the spirit indeed is willing, but the flesh is weak." At the ripe old age of ten, I was completely oblivious to the intense war between spirit and flesh that would tear me apart as I grew older.

We still had the cottage on Grandma's property, and the family went back and forth between Sydenham and the truck-stop. In grades five and six, I returned to Sydenham to finish my primary school there, which gave me friends in both places. Some nights I slept at the truck-stop and hitchhiked to Sydenham after morning chores. Other nights I slept at the Sydenham cottage or at a cousin's house that was nearby.

At the end of sixth grade, I returned full-time to the truck stop and attended Niddrie High School about ten kilometres from Keilor. I was fairly strong and fit and had become a good swimmer, so I joined the first form (seventh grade) swim team. I won the captaincy by a millisecond and got to swim the fifty-metre sprint against the Victoria State champion. I came in third in that race, but as a team we won the relay event, another fantastic memory. I still have the medal.

But my newfound fame at Niddrie High was short-lived, as after just a month there, Dad had to move north to Queensland for his health. The almost two-thousand-kilometre difference in latitude between Melbourne and Queensland meant that winters were far warmer up north, which greatly alleviated Dad's asthma. He'd spent the prior winter there by himself. This year he took me with him and John the following winter.

As Dad and I drove north across the plains, we ran into

trouble in the form of a massive sandstorm. As we could barely see the road, we pulled off to the side of the highway. After being parked there just a short while, Dad decided to get us out of there. Unfortunately, our tires had bogged down in the drifting sand. Dad kept revving the car, rocking it back and forwards furiously to try to free us from the sand. But all that accomplished was to tear the rubber off the wheels until the white lining showed.

At twelve years old, I had no idea why he was reacting in that manner. Jumping out of the passenger side of the car, I opened the driver's side door and yelled at Dad through the huge clouds of dust, "Stop it! You're wearing the tyres out!"

Reaching in, I turned the motor off, took the car keys and my sleeping bag, then lay down in the dusty country culvert and went to sleep, my head inside the sleeping bag. While I felt a bit guilty that my action was somewhat rebellious and disobedient, I also concluded this was the only way to preserve our vehicle. When I awoke, I was covered in thick dust as though someone had buried me in sand. Dad was inside the car, sleeping upright.

I've thought about that incident many times since. I eventually came to realize Dad was just trying to keep himself and his young son alive out there on the plains of New South Wales. Asthma and dust don't go together. Neither do heavy trucks whose drivers can't see parked cars in blinding dust storms when they come upon them. I'm sure Dad was just desperate to get us out of a dangerous situation, and my response didn't help.

4

A Second Taste

That said, we finally did make it safely to Brisbane, Queensland. Dad had arranged to manage a second-rate motel there temporarily. I bussed to the local high school and sold newspapers in the evening. Each paper boy had designated street corners and kept to those so as not to get into fights with other paper boys. I also had one hotel, which was lucrative. My particular newspaper was *The Telegraph*. I'd walk up and down yelling "Tele Paper City Final!" to let buyers know it was the final edition of the day.

After a few months, the motel job finished. Dad rented a house on a small island in the bay, which necessitated taking a ferry to the mainland, then catching the bus to school. I liked the island life, especially weekends when I could go swimming and laze on the beach. But school wasn't so great. I recall getting cornered in the toilets by a rat-pack of boys several years older who liked to pick on new kids.

To make matters worse, my school clothes didn't fit. Mum would buy good quality shorts and shirts and mail them to Brisbane to make sure I was properly clothed. Dad could have bought them, I suppose, but Mum wanted to make sure Dad didn't use the funds to buy Bibles or help some homeless person, then buy my clothes at a second-hand shop. But the clothes she sent were always too big, making me look even poorer than we were.

"Don't worry, son," Dad would assure me. "You'll grow into them!"

Financially, times were always tough up there. Looking back, I think Dad was embarrassed at the situation into which he'd brought me. But he also had to stay alive, which was the key purpose of being there. We all wanted Dad to live. And in truth, the lifestyle of poverty only worried me sometimes. Otherwise I saw it as one great adventure other kids didn't get.

Purchasing materials for homework assignments was something else our scant existence didn't always allow. One time I had to produce technical drawings for a metalwork class. Dad took me to buy the proper paper, pencils, and other necessary materials. I worked diligently into the night, determined to show the teacher my full value as a student.

The next morning, I boarded the ferry with my drawings sleeved in a cardboard folder. All was good on the island-hop as we picked up other kids on their way to school and made our way across the bay. Climbing from the ferry onto the jetty, I carefully clasped my expensive homework under one arm while using the other to balance.

Phew, I made it! I congratulated myself. *Mr. McClelland is going to be so pleased with me!*

But I hadn't made allowance for the wind, which was

considerably breezier at the top of the jetty than down on the ferry. As I walked in-land along the jetty, a powerful gust concentrated its full force on the tightly-held folder under my arm. I lost my balance—and my grip on the folder. With speechless disbelief, I watched my neatly-sketched drawings skitter like blown leaves across the bay, then sink below the waves and disappear.

Perhaps a normal reaction would have been to burst into tears. But after all we'd been through on this trip north, I just burst into laughter, thinking, *Mr McClelland will NOT believe this!* And he didn't. Thankfully, some schoolmates who'd been on the ferry testified to the plundering breeze that stole my artwork.

Toward the end of that year, Dad and I moved to a boarding house back on the mainland. That led to my second taste of alcohol. By now I'd turned thirteen. Another boarder was twenty-one years old. I was closest to his age of the boarders and got on well with him. One evening, he'd received an invitation to an official function and wanted a companion to go with him. He asked Dad if I could go, and Dad said yes.

The boarding house owner's son generously loaned him his beautiful four-year-old Jaguar motorcar with woodgrain dash and leather seats to attend this prestigious affair. We both dressed up in our best attire and sped off into the night. Beer flowed by the jugful at the event. I partook liberally, getting horribly drunk.

When I stumbled in after midnight, Dad didn't say a word

to me. Nor did he the next morning. But I'm sure he was disappointed and that he had a stern chat with my mate when the bloke recovered from his own hangover.

After just a few weeks, we left the boarding house and headed home to Melbourne for the summer. We stopped in Tamworth, New South Wales, Australia's country music capital, not to listen to music, but to deliver Christian pamphlets Dad had typed up and printed on a portable printer. My job was to run the streets placing the pamphlets in letter boxes while Dad drove the car. It was teamwork!

Our elderly second-hand FJ Holden had virtually no heating, and we had to hotwire it to keep it going. One icy morning about 5:00 a.m., Dad was freezing-cold and exhausted from driving but knew we had to keep going. I was really cold as well and trying to sleep huddled under a blanket. Desperately, he turned to me and asked, "Son, how'd you like to drive for a while?"

That was a different time period, and though only thirteen years old, I could already drive. But at 5:00 a.m. and ice-cold, I wasn't about to climb out from under that blanket, so I responded, "No thanks, I'm freezing here as it is."

Looking back, I know I should have exerted myself and helped him out. But at that age, you think dads are invincible enough to handle anything.

We had a good run with the car until we broke an axle not far from Jerilderie, a small town several hours drive north of Melbourne. While being towed into Jerilderie, I pressed Dad to let me hitchhike the rest of the way home as I wanted to get there in time to see my old classmates at the Sydenham Christmas concert. That was again a different era, and Dad agreed.

About 6:00 p.m., I caught a ride with an older immigrant man in a pickup van. I was at first suspicious of the driver, clasping Dad's leather Gladstone bag with my good clothes in it tightly against me as though it held gold booty. But my eyes eventually grew heavy, and I fell asleep. I awoke a few times and conversed with the driver, who turned out to be a nice man. He dropped me off at a big roundabout in Melbourne about 2:00 a.m. It was pitch-black except for a few streetlights.

From there, I walked and hitchhiked to Keilor, arriving at the truck-stop at about 4:00 a.m. As I walked past the truck-stop window to go around to the back gate, I spotted John inside in his pyjamas, just checking the shop with the lights out. I banged heavily on the glass door, scaring the living daylights out of him. After he let me in, we stayed up and made a milkshake, laughing together as I told him of our escapades. Then I went to bed and slept like a log. Dad made it home a few days later.

During the time period from Mum and Dad's purchase of the truck-stop to the Christmas I arrived home, my four older sisters had all married and moved away. With all the girls gone, Mum now needed a hand in the shop, so I stayed home and did school by correspondence. This was quite common for rural kids on remote farms, but not in suburban Keilor. In making her request to the correspondence school, Mum had explained our difficult circumstances with Dad ill much of the time and Mum needing help. They agreed to let me do the correspondence school. That next winter, Dad took John to Queensland and I stayed home to help Mum.

The first year, I did well enough at the correspondence courses that I won a scholarship. Mum was really pleased since that meant all my education for the next four years was paid for. But instead of using that opportunity to achieve a sound formal education, I talked Mum into letting me leave school at fifteen to work full-time in the family business. She was always exhausted and really needed the help, so she reluctantly agreed.

By this time, the Calder Freeway had been built around the back of Keilor, changing it into an even lovelier little village without the major highway running through it. To move with the times, Mum turned the truck-stop into a small general store with a take-out fast-food menu, which kept us just as busy.

For the next years until I was seventeen, I worked at the store split-shifts Monday through Friday, much of Saturday, and for ten to twelve hours on Sundays. While I provided needed relief for my parents and learned a lot about dealing with people, Mum worried about my long-term future. I felt a bit of shame too since most of my mates were doing well at school and crafting careers for themselves while I was just stagnating and going nowhere.

One bonus for Dad was that I could help him with his Bible-focussed work. Any time he had to go out for church meetings or other reasons, I would go too as his extra eyes, ears, hands, and feet. I also took one longer trip with Dad the summer I was fifteen to Swan Hill, Victoria, about a four-hour drive north of Melbourne. Dad wanted to do a forty-day fast and thought that might be a quiet, remote place to do it.

Dad took a short-term lease on a small timber house with high ceilings that made it cooler in the summer heat. There was a vegetable garden, which provided nutritious food for when he had completed his fast. To keep me occupied while he studied and fasted, Dad sent me to the local boxing gym where a lot of local aboriginal and other kids worked out with the bags and in the ring. I did the same for those few weeks and loved it.

Dad finished the fast, but it also nearly finished him. We packed up all our gear and began the drive home to Keilor. But the fast had left Dad so lacking in energy that he only made it ten kilometres before pulling over. He turned to me. "Here, son, you'll have to drive."

Unlike my response at age thirteen, this time I jumped at the chance. I drove the entire remaining distance to Keilor, arriving about 2:00 a.m. Dad was pleased to get home but also clearly spent. I felt invigorated.

5

Working And Drinking

I worked in my parents' store until I was seventeen and a half. I then got a job as a lineman with the government's telecommunications giant, the Postmaster General, or PMG. After a few years, PMG renamed itself Telecom, then later again Telstra, as we know it today. I worked installing and repairing phone lines, pits, and pipes in manholes and up ladders on poles.

It was a job I really loved, and in time after various roles in the company, it became my career. As one of the world's top communications systems, they were committed to high standards. Every pipe installed had to be at a measured depth. Every pit had to be level so people wouldn't trip over them on the footpaths. Community requirements had to be forecast many years in advance to ensure there would be sufficient cabling in new areas. I found the precision and thoroughness of it very rewarding.

As part of my training, I spent six months in Ballarat, Victoria, ninety minutes' drive west of Melbourne. During this same time period, Dad and Mum sold the shop with a plan to move to Bendigo in central Victoria for their retirement since it had a better climate for asthmatics. They'd purchased a lovely house opposite picturesque Lake Weeroona, not only for its beautiful location but because the house had a huge rear room that provided ample space for home church meetings and Dad's printing equipment. Dad would have been in his element.

It was during the ninety-day settlement period of moving our goods out of the shop and into the new house that Dad went into the hospital, which I mentioned earlier, for cataract surgery. Though a simple operation, it just proved to be too much for his deteriorated health.

One Friday night while he was in the hospital, I hitchhiked from Ballarat to the shop in Keilor, thinking I'd catch up with old mates. Instead, Mum told me Dad would like me to visit. I'd just hitchhiked in the dark from Ballarat, and I didn't want to do that again to the hospital. It occurred to me that if Dad was in the hospital, I could take his car and drive over.

I had no driver's licence, but I didn't hesitate to grab his car keys while Mum was busy in the shop. After driving to the hospital, I had a nice chat with Dad, asking about his operation and telling him how things were going at training.

I went back the next night, but this time I didn't take the car as I had a couple of mates with me and decided it was too risky to drive again without a licence. It was then I discovered that Dad had been moved to Intensive Care. After our short conversation, he fell back to sleep and I left. My mates and I stopped to buy some fish and chips, then hitched a ride on a utility truck, eating the hot food as we jounced about in the back.

When I finally got home, it was to find out that Dad had passed away since I'd said goodbye to him in Intensive Care. This was the first death of an immediate family member I'd gone through, and it gutted me so painfully I couldn't even mention his name or endure conversation about him for the next two years. Our deep bond hadn't always been obvious since like most fathers and sons we argued from time to time. I was a typical teenager who thought he knew absolutely everything while Dad was a wise father trying to keep me on the rails. It wasn't until he died that I realised how much he meant to me and that our unspoken father-son pledge to each other was melded together far stronger than I'd ever imagined.

Dad's death was even more shattering for Mum. Spiritually, Dad and Mum were as close as two people could be. Now this tragic turn of events left Mum retiring to a strange new town all by herself while trying to get over the deep pain of losing a devoted spouse. Living alone in this empty house, Mum regularly thanked God for telephones. At least she could stay in verbal contact with her children and other family.

After the funeral, I had to return to work in Ballarat. Once my theory training was completed, I was sent to my first works depot for on-the-job training. Port Melbourne, a wharf-side suburb, had a reputation for gangs, shootings, and a lot of criminal activity. Meanwhile, PMG workers had a reputation for high-standard work but also lots of hard drinking. At just eighteen years old, I didn't know what I was walking into.

It was in this job that I began drinking heavily. Prior to that, I'd been drunk a few times but wasn't a regular drinker. Now, depending on the work gang or team, we could always be found drinking at some time of the day or another, whether at lunchtime or later in the evening. Certain hotels in this area had tough reputations. I remember visiting one with my supervisor. As we walked up to the bar, I looked around at some of the other drinkers.

"Don't look at anyone twice!" my supervisor hissed at me.

"Why not?" I asked.

"Just one look that's okay," he explained. "But you take a second look or get fixated on one person, you'll have us both in a fight very quickly."

On another day, one of my workmates was having a quiet beer, minding his own business, when an argument broke out between two guys at the other end of the bar. As the yelling got louder, one of them ran for the door. The other guy pulled out a gun and shot him three times in the back. My workmate immediately put his beer down, turned away from the shooter so he couldn't see his face, then walked swiftly to the door, stepping over the body, never to return to that particular bar. Port Melbourne and South Melbourne were like that, and over the next two years, my workmates and I drank our way around their forty or more pubs.

Pay night was on Thursday, and that's when I first began drinking on my way home from work. I soon added Friday and Saturday nights. It wasn't long before I became a seven-day-a-week drinker. My wage was meagre, so I was often out of money. Having some great mates to drink with didn't help. Most of us had been friends for years.

To cut us all some slack, the culture of the day was for working people to go to the pub for a "liquid lunch," stop in again after work for a few beers, along with drinking on weekends. Most drinking men and women also drove under the influence of alcohol to some extent. They just did it more sedately than now. We would take the backroads.

I recall catching a train home from work one evening following an afternoon at the pub. I'd been drinking, fell asleep, and missed my station. It was a country train, and there were no returning trains for hours. I had to get off at the next station and hitch-hike back home. Coming home tipsy happened more times than I want to remember. My life was fine providing I didn't try to give up the alcohol. To be truthful, I actually enjoyed it.

Oddly, the last two things I would do at night, drunk or sober, were to read my Bible and pray. I loved God and wanted to fulfil my calling to serve Him, but there was an internal tug-of-war going on. The spirit that came with the alcohol was powerful and most times the one I favoured. I developed my routine of drinking first, then spending time with God. It sounds so hypocritical doesn't it? God's mercy and grace is never forgotten in my life.

During this time, I started surfing, which introduced another place full of fun, laughter, and alcohol—the Anglesea

Hotel not far from Bells Beach, Victoria. Despite the drinking and partying in which I participated, the final thing I did each night as I parked my wagon or van beside the sea to sleep was to turn on the internal light, read my Bible, and talk to God. This was not out of some feeling of religious duty but genuine enjoyment. Drinking while still attending church and Bible studies was like being married to two women, both of whose company I loved.

Other than that, the beach gave me some magical times. Along with other surfer friends in their vehicles, I would reverse my van toward the sea, open the rear door, and let the sea breeze flow through all night while I slept under blankets beside my surfboard. Some of us would rise at dawn for a surf, trying not to wake the others as we paddled quietly out so that we could have the surf to ourselves. The salt and sea air just couldn't be beaten to make you feel alive. We called the sea our "cure-all" as that first dip of your head under a wave not only energised the whole body but cured our hangovers. Of course in the winter, it was just plain freezing.

During the years when Dad had needed to go to Queensland for his health, John and I had become very helpful to both parents, tag-teaming so one of us was with Dad in Brisbane while the other helped Mum in the store. After Dad's death, we tag-teamed again. John moved with Mum to be with her in Bendigo for the first couple of years. I had to wait two years for a job transfer. I then relocated to Bendigo, staying there with Mum for the next three and a half years.

My drinking continued with new friends, both at work and socially. But so did my spiritual life. On Tuesday and Thursday nights, Mum and I would spend about an hour together in Bible study. I even got baptised in the middle of winter in the muddy waters of Lake Weeroona opposite our house. It was stingingly cold!

Our next-door neighbours, a lovely family who were very good to Mum, attended Creek Street Mission, a vibrant Pentecostal church with a great pastor. On midweek praise nights as voices rose and fell in beautiful harmony, it sounded as though an angel of the Lord must be orchestrating the praise. Sometimes I joined in, but more often I would stand there with my eyes closed, just listening and feeling the spiritual presence in the congregation.

At the same time, I still enjoyed both sides of the alcohol-spiritual fence and had no wish to give up either. Many times in those years, I drove the two-and-a-half-hour trip from Bendigo to Anglesea to surf, window down, blond hair blowing in the breeze, and my car stereo turned up as loud as it would go. I enjoyed those days on the beach with my mates while God was wanting my life to consistently follow Him.

But while both my social and church life were going great in my opinion, I was having trouble at work. Drinking after work and partying on weekends weren't conducive to hard work during the week, which left my supervisors with no option but to discipline me. My punishment was an odd one as they assigned me on various short-term teams that had me living away from home for the next twelve months, returning only on weekends unless I chose to drive to the beach. The living-away-from-home allowance actually doubled my wage. Some punishment!

Getting away from the Bendigo depot was helpful in one way as I worked under some sympathetic supervisors who saw value in me and gave me responsibility that helped me develop as a worker. I was determined not to let any of them down, and that responsibility helped me dig myself out of my hole and make something worthwhile of myself.

The downside was that I was living in hotels the entire year, which certainly didn't help my drinking. Every night of the working week except Friday, when we travelled home, our team would meet for drinks immediately after work, then shower and have the evening meal, after which we'd return to the bar, where we'd keep drinking and playing pool. Every week or two would see us in a new town and new hotel. Weekends, whether in Bendigo, Melbourne, or Anglesea, were the same.

After those fractured Bendigo years of church, drinking, and partying, Mum eventually received an offer from a motel group that wanted to buy some of the houses across from the lake. So we sold up and came back to Sydenham, where Mum built a new house next to one of her sisters just down the block and around the corner from Grandma's original house.

My drinking didn't stop or even slow down. I remember driving home one night after having a drinking session with mates at the Keilor pub. I felt so absolutely useless to God that

I was weeping as I prayed, *Lord, please don't run my car into a pole or tree and kill me!*

Later, I thought, *What a bizarre thing to pray!*

This type of real desperation is in more lives than we know. Despite the daily smiles and laughter I showed to others, I was perpetually disappointed with myself. Which begs the question of how disappointed a person has to be before their actions change. Small changes aren't so hard. But when you have a beast within you that is so entrenched it seems to be sown into your DNA, what do you do with that?

Of course there is prayer, and that certainly works. For me though, before God would answer that ongoing silent and sometimes audible prayer inside me, He wanted my decisions to align with his. This was difficult as alcohol had become so much a part of me that making a decision to give it up felt like asking me to cut off my right arm.

Some people during this period who knew my two opposing lifestyles called me a hypocrite. This stung like a bee-sting on sunburn. But the problem was much deeper than that. I had two extremely powerful forces within me pulling in opposite directions, each winning at certain times but the alcohol winning more often.

So was I a hypocrite? I think the word hypocrite should be used very carefully. I don't use it myself as I've met too many people like me who just struggled hard with stuff. I think God would prefer us to look for the deeper reason behind the so-called hypocrisy and try to help rather than just blurting out a judgmental insult. Anyone can do that!

6

Change Through Decision

A couple of years later, I got pulled over by the police. They administered a breathalyser. I blew over the limit, but thankfully not by much. This resulted in losing my driver's licence for a short time. It also resulted in my giving up alcohol cold-turkey. I was going to have to go back to court, and as a Christian I didn't want to lie to the magistrate if he asked me if I'd had another drink in the interim. I wanted to be able to look at him and say, "No, Your Honour!"

So that very night, I quit drinking. I was stunned it proved so easy. God was clearly involved. Did I pray to give up alcohol? No! The desire just left me after I'd made a firm decision with my heart. This was a decision God was pleased with and one He could be involved in. He took the craving for alcohol away immediately.

Amazingly, once the alcohol was out of my life, I found I could get on with God's work, and I did just that. For the next three years, I experienced a fantastic time of walking with God. It felt as though I was living inside a permanent Sabbath Day bubble. I made many Christian friends, went to Christian seminars and other gatherings, bought and listened to the right Christian music, threw out the wrong music, read and prayed more, and spoke to more people about God.

One major effect of my changed life was the relief it brought my mum. When I drank, Mum typically worried about me from the time I left the house at night to when I knocked on her door arriving home at all hours of the morning. I think she wore her knees out praying for me. She lived until she was ninety-one years old, so I can't be found guilty of shortening her life. But I sure gave her some worries.

It was during this time I joined Christian Surfers (CS). They held fortnightly meetings in a family residence in Melbourne. It took my mate Chris, another Christian surfer, and me almost an hour to get there from Sydenham. But the meetings and people were always worth the trip.

Some weekends we went surfing with the CS crew. Now and then, we'd hold Christian outreach movie nights at surf beach locations. I also attended the national Christian Surfers conference in New South Wales. It was a clean time in my life, and I lapped it up. One major highlight was a surfing trip to the surf mecca Cactus Beach on the Great Australian Bight. Six of us from CS plus a dog in three cars laden with surfboards and camping gear drove eighteen hours, stopping occasionally for a surf at some well-known beaches on the way.

Little did we realise when we stopped in Ceduna to buy two weeks' worth of food that the local community was in the middle of a severe mouse plague. Within three days of setting up our tents at Cactus Beach, mice had eaten through our food. We had to draw straws to see who would drive an hour-and-a-half back for more supplies. At breakfast in the kitchen tent, we sat on chairs holding our food in one hand and something to whack the mice in the other. One morning I counted fifty-four mice crawling over everything we owned, including our bags, food, and feet. We secured what we could but were fighting a losing battle.

When we weren't surfing or killing mice, we listened to Christian music and teaching on the car stereo, discussed Bible verses, or went on walks around the headland. Rick, the man running the Cactus outpost, invited me to have dinner with him on my own one Saturday night. Rick lived a spartan existence right on the beach in a stone house with a mixture of corrugated iron and glass windows he propped open with a stick for fresh air. The evening breeze rushing through the house was refreshing after a day's surf in the heat and salt water.

When I arrived, Rick had an open fire going with some basic pots and pans close by for easy use. Welcoming me in, he asked, "Join me in a beer, Niv?"

With my history, how did I explain without offending him that I was now a non-drinker? Aloud, I said, "No thanks, mate. I don't drink."

He shot the offer out again. "C'mon, surely one of my special homemade brews will be okay as a one-off."

I relaxed a bit and said, "Yeah, why not?"

With that, he poured ice-cold beer into two large glass

mugs. The heat from the day and chill from the beer created a frost on the glass I had to acknowledge looked refreshing and sumptuous. We sipped as we talked about life, dinner, families, and Jesus Christ.

"Where's the missus?" I eventually asked Rick.

"Oh, she's away at the moment," he responded.

The house seemed more like a bachelor lived there, so I assumed she'd been gone for some while. I felt privileged to have been singled out for an invite to this stone sea shack, especially since it was my understanding that Rick was in partnership with a famous Aussie surf movie maker. I was determined not to be one of those born-again Christians who hammered him about Jesus as I'd seen some people do.

Our dinner comprised of two good-sized fresh fish Rick had caught earlier in the day, seared and cooked to perfection on the open fire in a pan drowning in butter, sprinkled with just enough pepper and salt, and topped with a garnish of lemon and dill. As an accompaniment to the fish, Rick was preparing a variety of vegetables to be added to a pot of boiling water. He was standing at his cutting bench slicing carrots when an adventurous but foolish mouse darted across in front of him.

As if he'd done it a thousand times, Rick instantly dropped the knife he held in his right hand, grabbed the mouse, and whacked it head-first over the edge of the bench, killing it instantly. Throwing it in the bin, he picked up the knife and continued cutting the carrots without missing a beat in the conversation.

Oh, well, we are in a mouse plague, after all! I reminded myself. We ate, talked, and had another home-brew, which tasted as refreshing as the first one. Two was enough for me.

Our conversation meandered its way through various topics, yet it always seemed to come back to Jesus Christ. As with my dad, that was my favourite topic when I was doing well. We spoke about the existence of God, the Noahic flood, mankind's fallen state, and the redemptive blood of Jesus Christ. All life revolves around God, and I think Rick was beginning to realise that. He asked me about sin, all the wars the world has seen, and of course the usual question: "How can there be a God when there has been so much brokenness in the world?"

I sensed then he might be talking about his absent wife and their relationship. I was about thirty years old then and still single, so it didn't seem right to be giving advice. I just listened and spoke gently about how Jesus could heal all wounds. I don't know to this day whether Rick accepted Jesus Christ as his Saviour. I think he needed to chew over the information and digest it for a while.

A few months later and not due to Rick's homemade beer, alcohol re-entered my life, which swiftly destroyed my new testimony. On one single disastrous night in a cunning move by Satan, that deceitful spirit who wants us all to fail and die in hell, my teetotalling came to an abrupt halt.

7

Relapse

At this stage, I was working three jobs, my main employment with PMG along with part-time jobs, as I was trying to save up some extra money. One night of part-time work, the mate I was working for pulled his truck up to a bottle shop and asked, "Niv, would you like a can of gin and tonic?"

I thought it was odd he'd even ask but instantly replied, "No thanks, mate, just a Coke will do."

The next week I didn't see the devil coming. My mate pulled up at the same bottle shop and asked me the same question. But this time he added, "Come on, Niv, one won't kill you!"

For some strange reason I still don't understand except that Satan must have been working overtime, this time I responded, "Yeah, okay."

Within six months after consuming that cunningly delivered Trojan Horse dressed in a can, I found I was drinking more heavily than I had in earlier years. This time I'd really earned the title of hypocrite. Even non-Christian friends and fellow-workers were aghast, not believing what they saw. It got so bad that my pastor arranged to stay at my place one night after a function. I'd put the empty alcohol containers out in the garbage bin, but I couldn't put the spirit of it out.

When we prayed together the next morning, my pastor asked God to remove the spirit of iniquity from my flat. Was I embarrassed? You had better believe it! Did that make me give up? No!

This time around, I was a living disgrace with less hope within me than I'd had before. It took a collision to get me to stop this time. As I told someone not too long ago, "One drink didn't kill me, but it did kill my brother!"

I find that many men, women, and children struggle with all sorts of similar issues. When we dig deeper into people's lives, there seems to be a different person inside trying to get out of the one we see. They are all held captive by something.

Inside a fat body is a thin person or athlete. Inside a struggling businessperson is an entrepreneur. A singing star or great speaker lives inside an introvert, a good husband inside an angry man, a beautiful wife and mother inside the alcoholic woman, a respectable neighbour inside the drug-affected man. It may even just be someone wanting friendship inside the lonely recluse.

Many people can't figure out why they can't change into that other person who consumes so much of their mind-time. Despite the books, courses, corrections, diets, encouragement, beauticians, doctors, and psychologists, they still struggle with achieving that type of change. We are all only one decision away from success. But what is the true definition of a decision? Decisions become fruitless spoken words without active and consistent back-up. Depending on the problem, the length of consistency required to achieve permanent change seems as arduous as walking across the Sahara Desert in bare feet without water.

My situation may not be the same as for others. But I know this. For me to get prayer to work, I had to make a wholehearted decision. When I gave up alcohol the first time, it wasn't for the desire to give up alcohol. It was because I didn't want to tell a lie to that magistrate. I was unequivocally committed to that outcome. This established a foundation of truth within me. If I were only partly committed, it would not have been the full truth and the other side of me would still win.

What I see more clearly now is that my Christian life was never meant to be like a mixed drink where I stir some ingredients together with the Holy Spirit to obtain the perfect life. For as far back as I can remember, I have always believed alcohol and a godly life don't mix. I have always thought a godly way of life doesn't need alcohol. There is enough "spirit" in the Holy Spirit to satisfy every need and desire we will experience in our Christian walk. The Holy Spirit is capable of changing every part of our lives to overcome all obstacles and reach the heights of love to which God calls us, But only if that's what we *wholly* desire.

At the collision site when I was inside the car with John, time seemed to stop. In those seconds, I made some very fast but committed decisions about alcohol, my pathways, choices, lifestyle, and my upcoming marriage. I stopped drinking forever and crawled out that upside-down window a completely different person. When John died, an extraordinary sense of aloneness and profound responsibility flooded over me. It may sound odd now, but during those very few moments in the car, all I did was pat him on the back and say, "Sorry, mate!"

If that sounds cold-hearted or divorced from the very real world in which we lived, I meant it with all my heart and life. I knew I couldn't take him with me. He would never again be around to run things by or have a laugh with or even have him tell me off as older brothers do. I no longer had a big brother in my life. I had to leave him behind in that car along with my free spirit—the alter-ego John kept cautioning me about that had brought me so much trouble and that kept me thinking I could get away with living a double life.

It was some time after the collision during some personal Bible study that I better understood how Noah, after living such a God-approved life, got drunk when the pressure was off and did stuff he wouldn't have done normally. In doing that, he tarnished what had been a spotless existence and caused his son Ham to err in his judgment. Alcohol has a way of enticing us to drink just one or two more. We then begin losing our inhibitions and our judgment. My sense of judgment was replaced by something less godly. I wanted none of that anymore.

As I read the New Testament, the apostle Paul seemed to

caution me personally to not live for myself as I had been. Rather, my life was one to be lived for others. Paul's epistles also showed me that he understood people's weaknesses and that I shouldn't encourage those weaknesses by following my own desires, as he once warned the church in Rome.

> Therefore, let us stop passing judgment on one another. Instead, make up your mind not to put any stumbling block or obstacle in the way of a brother or sister. (Romans 14:13)

The trouble with alcohol is that nobody knows they have a weakness for it until they begin drinking. I was unaware at ten years old that a seed had been planted in me that would end up controlling my life. Not just the seed of alcohol but the seed of a carefree life that only really exists within the confines of a drug. Despite being responsible in most areas of my life, I always felt as I grew that I needed to escape it. I loved and sought the irresponsibility attached to alcohol. The unworried life was a major attraction, and at that stage I hunted it down whenever I could, morning, noon, or night.

I have no intentions of being that bad-seed planter for my own child or anyone else's life — child or adult. I guess that's another reason why even when I drank I didn't drink around Christians. Besides being ashamed of it, I wanted to keep those two camps very separate. I didn't want others thinking they could merge the two by seeing me do it. It wasn't that I ever thought the two *could* be merged. I was just caught in a hole. Plenty of people, including Christians, have damaged their bodies, lives, marriages, and even ministries due to alcohol, and many have died alcoholics simply because they started drinking without understanding the stickiness of that spider's web.

I believe today that alcohol would actually work against me helping others. A person seeking help might ring me. But that person would instinctively lose hope if they heard me slurring or tipsy on the other end. How could I pray with them or offer sound judgment from God? What if their problem was alcohol and they rang me for help, but I'd just finished three or four drinks and had a beer in my other hand when I took their call? How would that conversation go?

"Hi, this is Niv."

"Oh, hi, Niv. My name is Bill. Rob Smith put me onto you. He said you might be able to help me."

"Okay, Bill, what's the problem?"

"I'm a Christian, but I got myself caught up in alcohol, and I need someone who understands. Would you mind praying with me?"

"Hmm. Look, Bill. It'll need to be tomorrow. I'm just downing a few myself with some friends over a game. Is tomorrow okay? . . . Bill, are you still there? Hello?"

I never want to be guilty of being that kind of stumbling block if someone needs me. Life is hard enough for some people, and I might be the person God has placed in their path to offer support and guidance at that time.

8

Relationships

John and I and his wife at the time had purchased the garden supplies store five years before the collision. Because I was still working at PMG, now Telstra, John managed the business, growing it to a viable entity, while I occasionally worked there part-time. John had been married at this point for close to ten years, so he and his wife and I had signed a three-way business partnership and formed a registered company.

I was the only partner with cash up-front, which was how we were able to buy the business. John and his wife took out fairly extensive loans while I'd taken out a small additional loan on top of the cash I put in.

A year after we purchased the garden supplies, John's wife joined the police force. She was excited about this, but John was not. Becoming a policewoman meant spending lengthy periods away from home for training, assignments, and shift work. Also, the statistics for marital infidelity and divorce within the police force were extremely high.

Beyond these issues, police personnel at that time were not allowed to be partners in a business as this could possibly result in conflicts of interest. Some years later, this law was changed to allow police to hold a position in their own businesses. But at the time, John suggested his wife resign from the partnership as that would be the honest thing to do. She'd become a Christian long ago while they were dating, so he assumed she'd want to keep her slate clean with God and the police.

Instead, she chose to lie on her police force entry form and remain a partner. On top of that deception, within eighteen months she was cheating on John with a police colleague. By then she'd already moved out of the marital bedroom to a spare room under the pretext of needing more sleep due to her shift work. She'd also stopped sharing household duties such as washing clothes and cooking meals as well as marital intimacy.

All of these raised John's suspicions, but he didn't want to believe she would cheat on him. After discovering receipts for household goods that had never been delivered to their own home, he began following her. After several months, he tracked her to a house owned by the policeman with whom she was cohabitating.

Australian law at that time stated that if a married couple resided in the marital home separately—meaning they didn't sleep in the same bed, cook, wash, or clean for each other, or engage in marital intimacy—they were in a state of cohabitation but not as a married couple. After twelve months of such separation, one spouse could claim the home as their residence by simply changing the locks and effectively locking the other one out. A separation of assets would follow.

John's wife was nine months into this ploy when he uncovered proof of her infidelity. During this time, she'd often slept at her police colleague's house while telling John she was on assignment or shift work. One Saturday after discovering what was going on, John knocked on the door of the other policeman's house and requested that his wife come home. When she refused his pleas, cold reality set in that John had lost his wife completely.

John then did what he thought any self-respecting husband should do. He drove home, where he packed her clothes and a few other belongings into a suitcase and a large black plastic garbage bag. Driving back to her lover's house, he threw the suitcase through the front window, smashing the glass in the process, followed by the garbage bag. Returning home, he tore up all their wedding photos and threw them into the trash.

At the time, I was living in a flat in a Melbourne suburb close enough to the sea to hear the wind whistling through the yacht halyards as I drifted off to sleep at night. That Saturday was my day off, and I'd spent it racing on a friend's yacht. When I got back, I called John to see how he was doing. He told me what he'd done.

After all the months of suspicion and spying, having the situation out in the open was more a release of tension than anything else. Beyond John's state of depression over his wife, the past few months had been very difficult for our business.

The country was heading into a recession, and with all his marriage upheaval, John's heart hadn't been in the business, leading to a drop in revenue over the past year of more than twenty percent, something we couldn't afford.

To complicate matters, bank interest rates at that time were astronomical. Business loans averaged eighteen percent interest while overdrafts were twenty-five percent. Simply paying off their large loan and my small one while keeping the business afloat was difficult enough. Making any real profit was out of the question.

I decided to leave my career at Telstra to support John with the management role, giving him time to sort things out with his wife. This proved fruitless, and John eventually gave up hope of reconciliation and commenced divorce proceedings. Selling my seaside flat, I moved into John's house, both to keep him company and to make the sale funds from the flat available in case John needed them to buy his wife out of the business and personal assets.

I distinctly remember sitting one night with John, watching television. I could see the torment of his soul as he mumbled to himself and shook his head in disbelief at his marital situation. As a committed Christian marrying someone who was also supposed to be a committed Christian, John had never had any intention of becoming a divorce statistic. As far as he was concerned, his marriage was for life. This situation was about as wrong as life could get for him, and I felt his pain daily.

Yet in all his despondency, I never once heard John

denigrate his wife. He simply repeated, "She's my wife, and I love her."

John was the steady foundation of our business, liked by everyone who met him, always projecting a reassurance that things would be okay. If he were a ship's captain, you'd have the confidence he'd get you home safely. When I came into the business after leaving Telstra, I brought different skills. I convinced John to put some new strategies in place, including pushing sales and focussing on great customer service. From there the business began growing again. Within the next two-and-a-half years, we'd not only recovered our lost sales but doubled our revenue.

There's an old English quote: "Hell hath no fury like a woman scorned." John's wife wasn't happy about being caught in her infidelity or having her plot to seize their marital assets uncovered. By the time her lawyers wrote up her version of the story, John had gone from being a loving, devoted husband to a wife-beater. After the suitcase through the window incident, they didn't speak to each other for the next two years except through lawyers, which hurt John deeply.

Meanwhile, my own romantic life was going far better than John's. As mentioned, I'd been dating a wonderful Christian girl, Heather Milne, for the past several months. Long before I met Heather when I was in my late twenties, I'd prayed three brave prayers that impacted my future and hers.

The first was about wisdom and riches and where my true

desires should be aimed. I'd been reading King Solomon's prayer for understanding, which he'd prayed as a very young man shortly after becoming king following the death of his father, King David.

> Give therefore thy servant an understanding heart to judge thy people, that I may discern between good and bad: for who is able to judge this thy so great a people? (1 Kings 3:9)

What I noticed was that Solomon hadn't asked for money or riches of any kind, just internal riches for his heart and mind. I wanted that. I also read what Jesus had to say about the trap of seeking riches.

> And again I say unto you, it is easier for a camel to go through the eye of a needle, than for a rich man to enter into the kingdom of God. (Matthew 19:24)

I reread that verse a couple of times in the context of Solomon's prayer, thinking about what I wanted for my own life. I'd had enough trouble with other temptations without inviting one that was as hard to overcome as a camel going through the eye of a needle. Despite my many faults, I still wanted the Kingdom of God instead of getting bogged down trying to acquire this world's riches. So I prayed a modified version of Solomon's prayer for God to give me spiritual understanding and keep me from getting side-tracked seeking material wealth.

My second prayer was about a wife. A Bible passage from the book of Ruth stood out to me. Ruth, a Moabitess, was speaking to her mother-in-law Naomi, an Israelite whose family had moved to Moab during a time of famine in Israel (Ruth 1). Both their husbands had died, and Naomi was preparing to return to her home of Israel alone when Ruth expressed her commitment to stay with Naomi.

> Don't urge me to leave you or to turn back from you. Where you go, I will go, and where you stay, I will stay. Your people will be my people and your God my God. Where you die, I will die, and there I will be buried. May the Lord deal with me, be it ever so severely, if anything but death separates you and me. (Ruth 1:16-17)

While directed to a mother-in-law, this passage is often used in marriage ceremonies. I loved it from a prospective husband's view as I imagined a marriage built on this type of loving interdependence. My second prayer became, *Lord, this is the type of girl I want to marry!*

That said, I knew I had plenty of character flaws and that I had changes to make in my life if I was ever to become a man that a woman could love that deeply. I also wanted a wife who would think the world of me. I knew my second prayer wouldn't work without praying a third prayer, which was for God to remove from my life any other girl who wasn't His choice, however painful that might be for me.

God did just that, and it was indeed painful at times. In fact, it was seven full years from praying those three prayers that God brought Heather into my life. Considering all the time and money I was spending during that time on worthless pursuits such as drinking copious amounts of alcohol, I think the girls I was dating had lucky escapes. I wasn't ready for marriage at all.

Heather came from Nangiloc, a small farming community near Mildura, Victoria, which was about six hours northwest of Melbourne. When I met her, she was working at a plant nursery in Mildura. Heather knew members of my extended family from that region and had even gone to school with some of them.

My immediate and extended family had been wanting to see me married for some time. My Mildura area relatives who knew Heather couldn't think of a better woman for me. They cleverly arranged for both of us to attend an engagement party for one of my nieces. Once we were introduced, Heather and I immediately hit it off, smiling, laughing, and conversing easily together. I found her physically attractive and enjoyed her personality.

But despite our friendly interaction, I made no move to pursue a relationship with Heather. This perturbed my match-making relatives, who thought their cunning plot had failed. Not ones to be dissuaded, they invited Heather and me both to my niece's wedding a year later. We got along so well at the wedding that this time I did ask Heather out on a date.

I also ran the relationship by my pastor, who'd known her family for many years. He was so confident of Heather and her family he advised me simply, "Get up there and marry the girl!"

Four months later on Valentine's Day, 1990, I took

Heather on an outing up to a high hill overlooking the seaside town of Apollo Bay. Even after such a short courtship, we both knew we were made for each other. It was a beautifully sunny afternoon, and the hilltop offered panoramic views of the mountains, beaches, and coastline of Great Otway National Park. Kneeling down, I proposed to her. To my great joy and delight, she accepted.

We set a wedding date for Saturday, July 28, 1990, and began making wedding plans. I continued living with John and saved up money for the wedding. John was happy for me and excited about being my best man and seeing his little brother finally tie the knot. We could never have envisioned then that when the long-anticipated day finally arrived, John would already be seven weeks in his grave.

9

No Time to Mourn

By this point, things were happening so swiftly I didn't have time to mourn. I sat through many interviews and phone calls with police. The investigating police officer took statements from the two friends who'd eaten lunch at the hotel with me. He asked one of them what sort of person I was.

"A level-headed sort of bloke," my friend replied.

"Hot-headed," the investigator wrote down. Spotting what he'd written, my friend spoke up. "Hey, I said level-headed!"

The police officer made a correction. Sometime during all this, I rang the other driver I'd collided with. The man was healing from his injuries but for obvious reasons wasn't impressed with me. The newspapers reported that he was physically and emotionally scarred, which he certainly had reason to be. He'd actually borrowed the vehicle he'd been driving, now demolished, from his son.

The other driver would get fair-value reimbursement for the car from insurance. But I still felt terrible. Though my own funds were low as the country was in a recession, I sent the other driver some money so his son could put it towards his next vehicle. A small reparation for such an immense and unnecessary loss.

Just about a week after the collision, my mother received an odd phone call at 9:00 p.m. one night. The man calling said he was the person driving the car directly behind me all the way from the hotel. Mum asked him to call back in half an hour since I was still living at John's house several doors away and she'd need to ring me there. As soon as she did, I came over to her house. On the half hour, the man rang back.

"I saw the write-up in the paper and the way the police were trying to suggest you were driving recklessly," he told me. "I was driving behind you all the way down the highway, and I'm just ringing to say you were doing everything right. I noticed you coming to the turnoff, and everything was normal. As you had your indicator on to turn right and began slowing down, I passed your car on the left. Right then I glanced in the rear-view mirror. I couldn't believe it when I saw your car being flipped over."

An amateur in culpable driving, I figured witnesses might offset police claims of my reckless driving. So I asked the man to be a witness for me. He declined, explaining he'd been a witness to a vehicle incident once before, and the opposing legal team had shredded his testimony to bits.

"They weren't interested in the truth. Just to make me out as mistaken in what I saw. I couldn't go through that hell again, sorry!" The man went on to explain he'd only phoned to give me comfort that I hadn't been driving erratically.

It was indeed great comfort. Sometime after this phone

call, my bookkeeper rang me. Her seventeen-year-old son claimed he was one of three passengers in a car driving right behind the prior caller.

When I learned of these three new witnesses, I was desperate to get them to testify on my behalf. I met with my bookkeeper's son and got him to tell me his story. Every detail seemed true enough. The other caller had passed my car on the left, leaving the vehicle with this kid and his friends directly behind me.

"You were doing everything right," the kid said, just like the first caller. "We were going to turn right after you. But then you crashed."

I asked the young man if he and his fellow passengers would be willing to testify to what they'd witnessed. But like the first caller, they declined. They'd been in trouble several times with the local police and figured no one would believe their testimony. I was back to square one with no witnesses. Eventually, I learned I was a goner the moment I tested over the legal alcohol limit, so witnesses would have made no difference. But at least I had some consolation that I had not in fact been driving recklessly.

It didn't help that by then I was mired in another major conflict. After John's divorce, he and his wife had finally agreed on a settlement figure as many split couples do. At the time of his death, John was only two months away from completing the settlement, which would have left him free to get on with his life. In hope of the business picking up again, we'd even made several trips looking at prospective locations around the area to start a second garden supplies store once the recession was over.

But though a settlement had been made, John hadn't yet signed the divorce papers or made a will. His solicitor had reminded him several times of the urgency in getting this done, and he was always planning to get around to it, never factoring in the possibility of his own premature passing. Beyond my deep grief over losing my brother, this oversight created a huge dilemma for me after his death.

John's desire was for his estranged wife to receive only what was in the agreed settlement. But without the divorce decree or a will, she was technically still his wife so entitled to all marital assets, including the house, a spare block of land, shares in our business, trucks, loaders, even the Audi in which I'd had the collision as it was under John's name. Shortly after his death, she began making her claim on his side of the estate. Four months later, she was awarded the house, spare land, and John's personal bank accounts, though not the business at that stage.

By this time, Heather and I were married. At the time of John's death, I'd been living with him in his house for about a year, and Heather and I had been living there together since our wedding. The house was actually just three houses around the corner from my mum's home, and right next door to my grandma's original house. However, grandma had passed away by then, and another family lived there.

My sister Beth and her husband lived on the other side of John's house, while my mum's sister Elsie and her husband lived on the far side of my mum's house. You might say it was mostly one big extended family on that block—at least until John's ex-wife got his house and land. Then Heather and I moved out, and my ex-sister-in-law moved back in. Heather and I ended up renting a cheap two-bedroom half-house in Keilor Road, North Essendon, another Melbourne suburb about a twenty-minute drive from Sydenham. It was quite a dump. We removed two large truck loads of rubbish from the place, including a used porcelain toilet the owner had dumped among the overgrown backyard bushes. Wanting to turn it into some semblance of home for our new family, we brought in soil and made pretty garden beds with flowering plants.

Removing mould from the inside walls proved harder than the rubbish. We were forever scrubbing it off and disinfecting those areas. Heather suffered a lot of asthma while we were there, and we later found out that the mould was the cause.

Over the ten month period from moving into the half-house until my court case, we were robbed three times in the most bizarre fashion. I'm sure it would have been four had I not put preventive measures into place. I didn't believe these to be random robberies but figured John's ex-wife was after business files she knew I had. Back when we were still on good terms while she was married to John, she'd told me plenty of stories of different types of skulduggery from her experiences on the police force, so my scepticism wasn't totally unfounded.

The first time we were robbed, I was still managing the garden supplies store, and Heather was working there with me. We always drove to work and back in the same car. On this particular day, we arrived home in the evening after stopping to buy some groceries. I parked our utility vehicle in the small front yard. Gathering the bags of groceries out of the back, we walked past the tall rose bush and up the concrete steps to the front glass-and-timber door, which we discovered standing ajar.

Glancing at Heather, I put my index finger to my lips to signal for silence, then pushed the door open a few millimetres so I could see inside. The hallway was a mess of dumped and broken belongings.

"I locked this when I left this morning!" I whispered to Heather.

Concerned someone might still be inside, I set down the groceries and entered the hallway as quietly as I could, keeping my ears open and trying not to make the rickety wooden floor creak under the old carpet. Bracing myself for battle, I cautiously peeked around a few corners but soon satisfied myself that the coast was clear.

When we investigated further, we discovered that the thieves had jumped over the next-door neighbour's back fence, then over their side fence, before breaking in through one of our back windows. Along with stealing a few valueless items, they'd completely trashed the place. Every room was left a total mess.

I was immediately suspicious. That they'd targeted our

dingy little property and minimal possessions rather than the neighbours made no sense to begin with, especially since the neighbour who lived on the other side told us no one had been robbed in our housing strip during the past seven years he'd lived there.

Then paranoia set in, and I began wondering if John's ex-wife had used her police connections and resources to bug the place. She'd described to me how police place cameras and sound equipment in the strangest locations where residents would never guess them to be. Call it a touch of madness or whatever you like, but I figured maybe she'd done the same thing here. I searched in vents, under beds, in flower jars, behind photos and paintings, the bathroom, toilets, cracks in the floor, and every other possible place, looking for mini-cameras and microphones.

I also turned the stereo on before speaking to Heather. I left it on for the next several days and nights when we were home together and made sure all our conversations were kept low and near music equipment or the television. After a few days, I got sick of this obsession, and we went back to normal living. We'd contacted the local police the night of the robbery, and they came around to take statements. But I didn't mention my suspicions of John's ex-wife as I figured they'd think I was a madman.

10

A Show Of Force

The second time we were robbed, the thieves broke in through the back door, stole more items, and messed up the house again. I hadn't reinforced the back window after the last break-in, but I guess they thought I had, which might be why they'd kicked in the back door. Heather and I had returned from work in the same manner as the prior robbery when we discovered this break-in.

"Not again!" I exclaimed to Heather. As before, we contacted the local police, who came around for statements.

On the third robbery, the thieves turned the house into a shambles yet again. But this time they took several more valuable items, including Heather's engagement ring, which she'd left in a pocket of her dressing gown that was hanging on a hook in our bedroom. The ring was a beautiful old piece of jewellery made around 1910 of eighteen-carat gold with five small diamonds in a row. We'd found it together in a lovely store in the exclusive suburb of Armadale, Melbourne, and it had immediately appealed to both of us. It was the first seal of our life-long bond, so we were both very upset about its loss, especially Heather.

Meanwhile, I was becoming increasingly doubtful that these were random thefts. At this same time, John's ex-wife was pushing to take control of the garden supplies business. Since she'd never removed herself as a partner and now had John's share, that left me in a two-shares-against-one battle. She called a director's meeting at a neutral location, to which she brought lawyers as well as her common-law new "husband" for whom she'd abandoned my brother.

The meeting took place on July 18, 1991, five weeks before my scheduled court appearance. She started the ball rolling with an accusation that I was stealing cash from the business. To me it seemed she was taking advantage of her profession as a police officer to throw accusations around without evidence. In fact, there'd been no stealing. With the western world in a recession, we'd been barely making enough sales since John's death to pay current bills.

I'd brought my own lawyer, but we weren't far into the meeting before I realized I'd made a big mistake. I'd engaged a big-name Melbourne lawyer recommended to me by someone who'd used him in the past. His office was on an upper floor of a skyscraper so tall I could see a distance of about eighty kilometres through the floor-to-ceiling windows.

When I was escorted to a seat in front of his desk, I found the set-up very odd. Most legal offices I'd been in had masses of yellow manila files tied with string and marked up with brightly-coloured sticky notes. Other than a pen and notepad, the only thing on this man's desk was a business card holder with about thirty cards in it. As he offered me a seat, he introduced himself in an aristocratic tone. "I'm Alastair, and I work exclusively for one other client. Do you know who that is?"

Why would I know that? I wondered but chose not to say it aloud. Instead, I responded courteously, "No, I don't, Alastair. Who would that be?"

"I work exclusively for Kerry Packer."

I certainly recognized that name. The Packers were one of Australia's richest families. Glancing around the huge, posh office and enormous glass floor-to-ceiling windows with their incredible view of the city skyline and country-side in the distance, I had no problem believing his claim. But it set alarm bells ringing in my head. Why would a high-class bloke like this even consider taking on a small fish like me?

That set me thinking about what kind of fee this man would charge me. Cost-wise, I was clearly way in over my head here. I figured as soon as he realised how much money I didn't have, I'd be escorted out as quickly as I was escorted in.

But even as my hopes swiftly dwindled, I couldn't shake my curiosity. Why would he even consider taking on my case if he was playing around in the big pond of Packer calibre clients? I figured I had nothing to lose so I asked him outright.

"I find your case interesting," he replied.

As soon as the words left his lips, my case ran through my mind as quickly as figures in a tax office computer. I couldn't see anything interesting about it. To me, it was straightforward. Someone was trying to steal my business, and I was trying to stop them. His answer probably should have set even more alarm bells ringing. But then again, that may have only been my current acutely suspicious nature.

Instead, I answered with one of the most profound remarks I heard uttered that day. "Oh. Okay!"

I was still panicking about Mr Exclusive's price. I only had a certain amount of money to splash on legal fees, and when that ran out, his work for me would come to an abrupt ending regardless of how much was or wasn't done. I decided to take the chance, and we worked out the total sum I could afford. The meter started running as he asked a raft of questions and took detailed notes.

As we approached the meeting date, my expectations of work being done were increasing as speedily as the meeting date itself, but not much seemed to be happening. During the final week, I rang Alastair every night for an update. After all, I felt fairly exclusive myself now that I was running a close second to Kerry Packer.

But every time I rang him, he turned out to be intoxicated. At the meeting itself, he was clearly hung-over and sweating. When my ex-sister-in-law's lawyers started throwing ammunition, he didn't seem to know where he was with any of it. He argued back with all sorts of laws, statutes, and precedents, but he might as well have been talking to a group of fenceposts.

John's ex-wife's legal representatives weren't interested in the rule of law or the company's constitution but in seizing the assets regardless. The entire meeting was farcical and ended abruptly once the lawyers thought they got their points across. Two hours after the meeting ended and right at closing time, John's ex-wife showed up at the garden supplies store with her policeman common-law new "husband," four senior sergeants who were detective friends of hers, and two local police. Calling me a thief again, she ordered me off the property.

Looking around at the real thief and her goon squad of so-called heavies, I felt like a coiled snake ready to strike. Thankfully, I thought better of it. Heather and our other employees were still present, and I needed to keep myself as composed as I could under the circumstances. After all, this was a legal issue we were battling, and there might still be some small glimmer of hope up ahead.

What made all this more discouraging was that I felt I was taking on the entire police force, not just a couple of greedy officers. Looking over this entire small army of police personnel my ex-sister-in-law had dragged onto the scene, I felt defeated but still wound up. On the one hand, I'd placed myself in God's hand, whatever the outcome of this situation might prove to be. On other hand, I still had to go through the processes and emotional roller-coaster that went with them.

I went peacefully as the police escorted me out of the business I'd worked so hard to bring back to prosperity. Not that I had much choice since the officers had a police van there ready to haul me off if I caused any trouble. I was now in a no-man's land. Without the business, I had no income. There were only five weeks to go before my court case, so I couldn't really go out and look for another job. My wife was three months pregnant and now also without a job. Beyond all that, I still had business battles to fight.

I felt like one of those caged tigers you see at the zoo pacing around their compounds looking for a hole in the fence. Despite no holes being there, they still pound their circuits going over the same areas, thinking the opening to their freedom might be somewhere on their next round. I was doing that. At night, I found myself scrounging through legal books, marriage acts, director's manuals, and everything else that might hold a grain of hope, looking for the legal loophole everyone else must have missed.

In my gut, it just seemed that the entire situation was wrong and terribly unjust. That someone could be living as the *de facto* common-law wife of one person while at the same time claiming the estate of her ex-husband on what seemed a technicality of paperwork didn't seem right regardless of what the lawyers said. Unfortunately, what was moral and ethical just didn't seem to be the same as what was legal!

11

County Court And The Astute Judge

My final court case was scheduled for August 27, 1991, almost fourteen months after the collision and thirteen months after Heather and I were married. I had a strong suspicion the "thieves" might take advantage of our absence that day, so I arranged a friend to mind the house while we were in court. I asked my friend to keep the window blinds down so the thieves wouldn't know anyone was home and we might catch them in the act.

As I'd anticipated, at 11:00 a.m. when we were all in court, the phone rang at our home. My friend mistakenly answered it, thinking we might be calling from the courthouse. She heard only silence on the other end of the line. This went on for several seconds, then the caller hung up. When I learned about this later, I had no doubt the caller had been checking to see if the house was empty and that we'd been saved from a fourth break-in.

As I sat stoically in the dock of the court, dressed in a fancy Hugo Boss suit and tie I'd purchased specifically for my court appearance, a team of character references took turns making their way to the witness box. Each testified to my good character, what a great community-minded person I was, and how deeply sorry I felt over the accident. We were all hoping the judge would focus on my general exemplary behaviour and assess the accident as a one-off mistake. In truth, my witnesses made me sound so good I'd have let myself off and even apologised for asking such a model citizen as me to attend court.

I wanted to cry out to the judge, "Your Honour, release me with a warning, and it won't happen again!"

Surely the judge could see the truth of that and the sincerity of my repentance! But instead of responding as I hoped, he leaned forward in his ornate chair, looked sternly at me over the top of his glasses, and said in a sombre tone, "Everybody is sorry when they get caught."

Ouch! I felt the truth of those words as though God Himself had picked them out specifically for me. Everybody *is* sorry when they get caught, but only because they got caught. That judge had seen right through me as though looking through a clear glass window. Yes, I'd changed since the collision. Yes, I was a completely different person. I was hoping the judge could see I was no longer a threat to society who needed ongoing punishment.

But my whole life wasn't on trial. This court case was for a specific collision I'd had while under the influence of alcohol. I was on trial for what I'd done in just a split second of time, and the judge was right. I hadn't been sorry thirty seconds before the collision nor even fifteen or ten seconds or even one second. I was only sorry afterwards while hanging upside-down and watching the swift demise of my only brother. And for those few illegal moments I'd still been hoping to get away with, the judge needed to dispense suitable justice.

The judge finished rendering his verdict, a fifteen-month minimum sentence. Then his judge's hammer slammed righteously down on the bench, sealing the next part of my life. With the trial over, I was handcuffed, then escorted past my wife, mother, lawyers, as well as my brother's ex-wife, who was sitting there taking copious notes. There was no opportunity to hug or kiss my wife or mum goodbye. They just hugged each other in consolation, tears pouring down their faces, as I was led out of sight.

I was so deeply thankful that Heather had Mum and other family members for comfort, especially going through pregnancy as she was without her husband at her side. She'd got on well with my entire family from the moment she arrived in Melbourne, and they all loved her like another sister and daughter. In fact, from the time I went into prison, my sister Beth made sure one of her daughters always slept over at our house unless Heather had other visitors staying so she wouldn't be alone at night. At the time, Heather hadn't felt this was necessary, but in hindsight she saw that it kept her from becoming depressed and lonely. For my part, I was pleased she had company.

Once outside the courtroom, I was led to a stainless-steel lift that ferried me down to several holding cells deep in the bowels of the courthouse. There I took a seat on a long stainless-steel bench and looked around. I was not the only sentenced criminal down here on this brief stopover to prison, and once I'd given the others a quick glance, I kept my eyes averted and my mouth shut. The only prison I'd experienced so far was in the movies, which gave a less than salubrious depiction of prisoner relationships. Right then and there, I made the live-or-die commitment to myself that I'd fight to the death before I became some big oaf's boy-toy.

From the holding cells, all of the prisoners were escorted to a prisoner delivery van, which resembled a large stainless-steel box on wheels. It had slit windows near the top, far too high for anyone to see out since we were all handcuffed to the seat in front of us.

Looking to my right, I realised, *I've seen that guy before!* Then I remembered where. He'd been on the front page of the main newspaper after shooting a hotel bouncer to death in a car park. *Hmm, I'm in great company here!*

Going back to those mysterious break-ins, a few weeks after I was sent to prison, some of the more valuable goods taken during the third break-in were recovered just as mysteriously. Heather was informed they couldn't be picked up from the police station until a certain date. The day before that date, a plainclothes detective came to the front door of our home. When Heather answered the door, he demanded bluntly, "Are you Heather Neyland, and did you get your engagement ring stolen?"

He hadn't yet identified himself as a detective, so Heather naively assumed he was an insurance representative there to get further details of the stolen ring. She immediately responded, "Oh yeah, I'll go get the paperwork."

Leaving the man standing outside the front door, Heather walked across our lounge room to a filing cabinet where the insurance paperwork was kept. Taking out the paperwork, she turned to walk back to the front door. That's when she discovered the detective had silently followed her inside and was now inches away, towering over her menacingly.

As a twenty-five-year-old pregnant woman alone in the house with this large, brazen man, Heather felt immediately threatened and quickly manoeuvred to move their interaction back outside. Before leaving, the detective gruffly told Heather that her engagement ring was not at the police station where the other recovered property was being held. If she wanted it back, she'd have to go to the police station where my brother's ex-wife worked and ask for her personally.

Heather did exactly that. My brother's ex-wife told Heather she'd made a deal with the thief who stole it, adding in an intimidating tone, "You'll appreciate how hard I worked to get this ring back for you. Now, you are in possession of certain items I need to run the business. So maybe you can help me in this matter."

Heather was shocked at the implied demand for a quid pro quo to get her belongings returned, something completely inappropriate from a police officer as well as illegal. But she responded with artful innocence, "Well, all that stuff is with the solicitor. I'd need to speak with him about that."

Heather left the police station with her ring, and that was the end of the matter. No explanation was made as to why my brother's ex-wife had the ring in her possession, where or how the property had been recovered, or who they'd recovered it from. All of which strengthened my suspicions that my former sister-in-law was the real person behind the thefts. Now that I was in prison, and Heather had informed my brother's ex-wife that all the paperwork was with the solicitor, no further break-ins occurred over the next four years we had that house.

One important measure Heather and I had put in place from the moment she'd turned on us was to pray for John's ex-wife. Our prayer was that she would come back to her commitment to follow Jesus Christ, which she'd clearly abandoned. But a secondary objective of this prayer was to keep bitterness out of our own hearts. We didn't want any hostility toward John's ex-wife to take root in us as can so easily happen. Praying together had worked well, and Heather and I had been able for the most part to release our anxieties to God without resentment or indignation.

We'd also prayed together and as a family about the court case, and I'd also prayed personally and honestly that the judgment, whatever it turned out to be, would be God's will for me. As King David had done after his foolishness with Bathsheba (2 Samuel 11, 12), I threw myself on God's mercy, committing myself to accept without question whatever happened.

Despite my sincere prayers, I hadn't really expected a

prison sentence, though my legal advisors had. Subconsciously, I'd figured that because I had a pregnant wife, a frail mother who'd lost her only other son, and business battles still to sort out, God would allow me to go free with maybe some other type of penalty.

But He didn't. Instead, God pronounced a jail sentence on me. Not for a second at that time did I think I needed incarceration. But as my story began to unfold, I discovered that I certainly did. Prison would reveal weaknesses and strengths in me I didn't know I had. Dad used to say to me, "Look closely at your faults and fix them." I'm still fixing some!

While my original sentence was for fifteen months in prison, due to sentencing guidelines at the time, I automatically received a reduction to serve just ten months. When I learned the final sentence was ten months, a light started to shine on the dark pathway I was treading. Bible study had taught me that in Scripture the number ten stands for responsibility. For instance, Noah was the tenth generation from Adam and had the responsibility of remaining righteous, building the ark, and propagating the new world after the flood.

For much of my life, I'd tried to escape the constraints of responsibility, looking for freedom everywhere, something that hitchhiking and alcohol both gave me. I was not a Noah or anyone famous for that matter. But God wanted ongoing responsibility out of me from this point on, and ten months in prison was part of His training program to instil responsibility into me. I'm not saying that God killed my brother to put me on this path. God doesn't create temptation or the tragic situations that come about when we give in to temptation (James 1:13-15). But God does use and redeem sinful choices and tragic situations for His own glory.

12

The Dawning: Pentridge Prison

I'd been assigned to serve my sentence at Her Majesty's Prison Pentridge, more commonly termed just Pentridge Prison, which was located in Coburg, Victoria, a suburb about ten kilometres north of Melbourne. The prison was actually closed down in May 1997, just six years after my time there, and the area is now a housing community. But at that time, anyone driving into Melbourne via Sydney Road couldn't help but notice this massive stone monument to crime and punishment rearing ominously against the Coburg skyline.

A notorious hellhole throughout much of its history, Pentridge was founded in 1851, the same year my ancestors immigrated from Ireland to Newport, Victoria, to make a new and better life for themselves. During almost a century and a half of service, some of Australia's most infamous criminals were imprisoned there, including the Irish folk hero and outlaw Ned Kelly. It was considered a high-security prison, and the prisoners were used for hard labour, especially quarrying bluestone for the construction of roads. Which led to its colloquial nickname of "Bluestone College," so called because its inmates certainly did get an education there!

Pentridge consisted of a large compound occupying what would be almost an entire city block. High, thick bluestone walls surrounding the compound were topped with razor wire. Various facilities housed different types of inmates with varying levels of security. As the van passed through the main gate, it paused over a pit so it could be checked inside, outside, and underneath for anything that shouldn't be there.

The prison officers then opened the van's rear door and unshackled the passengers from the seats. Once we'd all clambered out of the van, they led us into a large area called D Division, which was where most prisoners started their prison life when they entered the Victorian criminal detention system. It was also where Ronald Ryan was hung, the last person in Victoria to receive the death penalty.

From there, depending on their classification and the population of other prisons, inmates were dispersed throughout the system. I'd been classified as a C, which was a low classification for less violent crimes. This meant I'd be spending minimum time in Pentridge and the rest on a prison farm. Because they were much lower security, prison farms were where most low-classified people were sent along with more serious offenders nearing the end of their sentence.

We newbies were in civilian clothing while residents were in their prison greens. We were all free to move around and chat in the processing area. There were even self-serve coffee fixings. Another newbie looked at me while mixing himself a cup of coffee and asked, "Don't I know you from somewhere?"

Unsure whether the question was genuine or he was just testing me out, I figured a rejection would be the wise response. Giving him a hard glance out the side of my eye, I said brusquely, "I don't think so, pal!"

My harsh response brought a fearful expression to his face. He apologised quickly and walked away.

Well! I told myself, *that worked!*

Another newbie, a skinny bloke in a black tee-shirt and tight black jeans, introduced himself to me as Nugget. We made ourselves some coffee and started chatting. He seemed a nice enough bloke, but his conversation was only too familiar in one sense. The underlying theme was how we all think we can get away with it—whatever "it" is. For me, that had meant driving above a .05 blood alcohol level when all the police signs were saying DON'T.

For Nugget, it had been an attempt to rob some 7-Eleven stores. Initially, he'd only wanted to rob one of them. But, as he explained to me, there'd been too many people at the first two stores, so he kept going until he found the right one.

To me, Nugget seemed a typical small-time criminal. He'd had plenty of opportunities to work an honest job but had simply chosen an easier, dishonest lifestyle. Many inmates are guilty of that. If they'd work an honest job, they might earn less or more slowly, but it would be safer and a whole lot better for them in the long run. They'd be able to pay taxes to help the safety net for their ageing or out-of-work family members, put some money in the bank for savings, and become another valuable member of society. But they need basic self-preservation smarts and/or some good character to make that happen, and many for a multitude of reasons lack precisely that.

Nugget had carried out his crimes with a mate and his girlfriend. The mate was the getaway driver behind the wheel of a Ford Falcon. Beside him was Nugget's girlfriend while Nugget sat on the passenger side with a shotgun. He had no plans to use the shotgun. In fact, it was empty. But the people in the store wouldn't know that, so he carried it for the bluff value it provided.

When they pulled up at the first 7-Eleven store, Nugget got out of the car with the shotgun and walked toward the automatic glass entry doors. As the doors opened, he saw too many people inside for a safe robbery. Turning around, he walked back to the Ford Falcon and climbed in. Nugget's getaway driver then headed to the next 7-Eleven in the hope there'd be fewer people in this store. As they arrived, Nugget once again got out of the passenger side and walked to the store, gun by his side. The automatic doors opened wide, and he saw that this store also had too many people.

"Darn it!" he muttered under his breath.

Off sped the Falcon to the third and final 7-Eleven. This time Nugget was in luck. Walking in, he wielded the empty shotgun, handed the attendant a bag, and demanded that it be filled with all the money in the cash register. The attendant obliged quickly, and Nugget left the premises with a bag full of cash. The Falcon raced off again into the night, this time heading for home so they could count the booty and decide what to do with it.

But they hadn't figured on one hiccup. At the first 7-Eleven, which Nugget didn't rob, the attendant had spotted a suspicious bloke carrying a shotgun and rang the police. At the second 7-Eleven, which Nugget also didn't rob, the attendant had also spotted Nugget and rang the police. Both times giving the Ford Falcon's car registration number to the police as well. When these would-be small-time criminals pulled into their driveway, thinking they were home free, the police pulled in directly behind them.

Leaping from the car, Nugget raced for the back fence. But he didn't get far before a burly policeman who could seemingly run the hundred metres in about five seconds grabbed his legs, bringing him to the ground in a classic rugby tackle. Nugget's aspiring criminal career was clean-bowled without making a run. He was handcuffed, fingerprinted, and marked for life simply because he hadn't wanted to work for a living. A good bloke, but I wouldn't take financial advice from him.

In the process of learning Nugget's story, I also received my cell number and a duffle bag with some odds and ends from the prison officer in charge. Still in my Hugo Boss suit and fancy Florsheim leather shoes, I was led to my first night's incarceration.

Besides the clothes I was wearing, that duffle bag contained everything I owned while in prison. All inmates are given one. If you left something behind in a cell as you vacated it, if you forgot to put it in your bag, it would most likely be gone when you came back for it. I learned to carry my bag everywhere and keep everything I owned within it.

From this experience, I've come to understand a bit more the mind-set of vagrants when we see them rummaging through bins and selecting all sorts of discarded junk they think is valuable. A couple of weeks into my sentence, I recall finding a small plastic bag and a rubber band on the floor. I instinctively stuffed them into my bag in case they became useful later. For what, I didn't know.

Like a typical Aussie, when I first came into the system, I called the prison officers "mate," not realising the required etiquette. "G' day mate! . . . Yes, mate! . . .No, mate!"

One officer had enough of my casual attitude to the hierarchy. Furiously, he yelled at me, "DAMN IT. CALL ME MISTER, SIR, OR BOSS! I AM NOT YOUR MATE!"

"Oh, okay, sorry, mate! Oops, I mean boss."

It was still winter when I arrived at Pentridge Prison, and there was no ducted heating within those two-feet-thick bluestone walls. I just about froze to death that first night. At this point, I didn't care about taking it one day at a time. I was just sensing my way through one minute at a time, keeping my eyes open, my mouth shut, and making sure I at least looked like I knew what I was doing. It was a time of apprehension and reflection.

That first cell was what they call a two-outer, meaning it had two beds in it. It had bare bluestone walls on three sides with a built-in plyboard cupboard with no drawers at one end to put a TV on if you were fortunate enough to have one. The fourth side, of course, was prison bars.

It also had a Brasco, which is a prison term for toilet. I quickly learned the unwritten cell etiquette regarding the Brasco. It is recognised as poor manners to expect your cellmate to hold his nose and turn his head while you do your business. So you do your ablutions, the heavy stuff, that is, at the general-use toilets outside the cell before evening lock-up. In a joint cell, unless you are sick, the Brasco is only for urine.

Thankfully, that first night I was put in with Geoff, a great bloke from Mildura, with whom I got on very well. We were both new to prison, and my wife is from the Mildura region, so we found plenty to talk about. I only spent a couple of nights with Geoff in D Division. But we kept bumping into each other as we went through the system.

13

The Realisation

Waking up each morning in prison is different from the outside. You couldn't simply get out of bed and head for the cornflakes. Or shower. Or even walk outside to smell the fresh air. Oddly, during my stay there you could light up a smoke in your cell as these were the days before smoking was banned.

If up early, you could have a pee in the Brasco, but quietly as the bloke in the other bunk might still be asleep. You then waited quietly, reading a book or old newspaper, hoping your cellmate woke up soon. About 7:45 a.m., the prison officers unlocked the cells and checked that we were all still there. They didn't want any Shawshank Redemption escapes.

Some cells unlocked automatically. Others were unlocked by prison officers with keys walking up and down the tiers. A stampede followed toward the toilets and showers. Breakfast was at 8:00 a.m. with lunch at 11:00 a.m. and the evening meal at 3:00 p.m., followed by lock-up at 4:00 p.m. All work and breaks were squeezed into this limited timeframe.

Then for the next sixteen hours, we were locked in our cells. The drudgery of that existence repeated itself seven days per week. Sixteen hours was a long time to be cooped up in a small room with only an electric kettle, toilet, TV, and someone you'd just met. There was a dirty window high on the rear wall of each cell, but these were mostly jammed shut by paint, time, and swelling timber.

All cells had steel bars over the windows, but the cell entrance varied. Some had steel bars for doors like the old western movies where the entire inside of the cell could be seen from opposite cells or walkways. Others had thick wooden doors with a small opening in the middle called a trap. At certain times of morning and night, prison officers would do a walkaround, calling loudly as he went past the door, "Hands on traps!" Each inmate would then place one hand on the trap so the prison officers could make sure the right number of inmates were in the cell and check them off against their list.

After those first two days with Geoff, I had a number of two-outers with different blokes, then I was moved into a four-outer. My cellmates there were decent blokes too. These weren't always the same men, but were constantly coming and going depending on transfers, release dates, etc.

One guy I shared a cell with was named Darren. He was the type of person who didn't trust anyone and felt he needed to be ready to defend himself at all times. He carried a homemade shiv (knife) in his underclothing during the day and slept with it under his pillow at night. This wasn't his first time in prison, and I was thankful when he left the cell as his demeanour and over-awareness were oppressive. But other than Darren, I had a pretty good run of cellmates.

Most inmates doing a long prison stint prefer that their fellow prisoners do their time quietly and get along with people. Young guys coming in full of attitude tend to get sorted out quickly. One young skinny kid about nineteen or twenty years old came in wearing a pair of high-end Adidas and with an arrogant posture. The next time I saw him, he had a black eye and a pair of cheap Dunlop KT-26 runners. Another inmate had clearly decided the Adidas looked better on him than on the skinny newbie and decided to swap without asking.

Like all the other newbies, I initially spent my days in one of D Division's three yards. These compounds housed inmates during the day who were either waiting to get a job or preferred not to have one. In some of Victoria's prisons, you had the choice to work or not to work. The payment is minimal but provides funds to buy small items from the prison canteen (commissary). The prison itself relied heavily on the work of inmates. Breakfast, lunch, and dinner had to be made, delivered, and the dishes washed up. Cleaning and laundry needed to be done as well as other services to keep the prison working.

The yard areas were all different shapes surrounded by high bluestone walls, which allowed the guards full view of what went on. The toilets in the yards were lined up in a row with only a waist-height brick wall to keep other inmates from seeing anything below your waistline. This gave some sense of privacy, but the prison officers perched above the walls could see everything. I felt so exposed I ended up using those toilets only once. They were also often blocked and overflowing.

Murderers, rapists, hitmen, white-collar thieves, as well as run-of-the-mill petty criminals all mixed together in the yards like a hazardous cocktail. This volatile mix often led to trouble. If I was reading a newspaper or book, I would always keep my eye glancing under the page to see whose feet were walking toward me.

I remember one guy about my age sitting down next to me and striking up a conversation. I joined in briefly until he mentioned he'd just come down from Queensland and when he got here he'd done "a few burgs to get me by." I left him sitting there. Burg is short for burglary, and my home had just been robbed several times so my fuse was short for petty thieves.

Many inmates didn't want to work, so they stayed in the yards, brewing up tea and coffee all day in an attempt to stem the boredom. The Bible says that idle hands are the devil's workshop (Proverbs 16:27 TLB), and that was certainly the case in the yards. So I got out of there and into a job after just four days, which was how long it took for my blood test to come through. Certain jobs like the kitchen required testing clean for diseases.

I would have liked a kitchen job, as I'd been told that was a great place to work. But my first assignment ended up being a billet in F Division, the protection yard. This was where inmates convicted of more vile crimes were sent, such as child molesters, rapists, and the like. Mainstream prisoners, who largely had an intense distaste for sexual predators and crimes against children, called it the "dogs" yard or boneyard.

Hating paedophiles is a strong and even praiseworthy code within the prison system. But this also makes it difficult for repentant paedophiles to leave their former life behind and try for a new future. As soon as anyone hears about their crime, they tell others within the prison, and the life or welfare of the ex-paedophile is now on the line. I used to feel the same way about such predators. But I've since come to know a number of former paedophiles and other sex offenders who have genuinely changed and live reformed lives.

My job in F Division included sweeping, mopping, cleaning toilets, serving food at mealtimes, and clearing up afterwards. The meals were wheeled on large trolleys from the kitchen to all areas of the prison. The food was reasonably healthy, such as corned beef with vegetables followed by a simple dessert. Once the meals were finished, I cleaned up my area, and the kitchen billets returned with the trolleys to pick up the empty dishes. I had that job for eleven days and was paid $28 per week. It was a good job, but the best part was that I could use a real toilet with a door during the day.

My next occupation in this stone castle of correction was a kitchen billet, which a cellmate had suggested I apply for since I was a "cleanskin," i.e., no drugs. When I got the job, I thought I had made the big time. But all new kitchen hands had to start at the bottom, which meant washing dishes.

This wasn't washing crockery in a normal kitchen sink. A huge room was piled floor to ceiling with large commercial stainless-steel cooking containers of all shapes. My role was to get them shiny again. This meant standing there in gumboots wrestling a long hose that writhed in my hands like a python trying to escape as it shot out a high-pressure stream of boiling water.

For cooking utensils and smaller dishes, there was the deepest sink I've come across. This water was also boiling-hot. Though I wore long rubber gloves, the water often leaked over the top of the gloves, scalding my arms.

Another inmate had been assigned to washing dishes with me. But like the Scarlet Pimpernel, he could never be found where he should be. He'd wander off for hours at a time to look up his various mates within the prison, leaving me to wash the pile by myself. I stuck by the code that you don't lag anyone in (report them to prison officers). This became a two-edged sword. On the one hand, it warmed me quickly to other kitchen inmates. On the other, I was left doing a two-man job much of the time.

That job became increasingly difficult since I suffered from eczema on my feet, which was aggravated by working all day in wet gumboots. My feet were red-raw and bleeding most of the time, and the constant itch from ankle to toe was driving me crazy. During this same time, I lost a filling in one of my back teeth. I'd been chewing on a toffee, and the sticky, brown rectangle of suction proved strong enough to pull out the filling. The nerve left exposed was as raw as my feet so that every breath of cold air made my eyes roll back.

I went to the Circle, the central location from which the prison officers administered their duties, and requested a visit to the dentist. They told me the dentist had been there the day before and wouldn't be back for two weeks. Explaining my dilemma, I asked for some Panadol to ease the pain.

This is just basic paracetamol one can buy over the counter, not morphine or oxycodone that might give you a high. But because it was still a drug, they only gave me two capsules, the painkilling power of which lasted for only a few hours. Then I was back to square one with an exposed live nerve. They did eventually give me a few more Panadol, but that fortnight went very slowly.

When I finally got to see the dentist, I saw one inmate's name scrawled all over the walls of the prison dental clinic, something I'd been cautioned by other inmates never to do. There was an unwritten saying in prison: "If you write your name on the wall, you'll be back to scrub it off." What this means is that if you think you're a tough guy for going to prison, which is typical of those defiant and stupid enough to sign their own name to their graffiti, you'll keep coming back until you've learned your lesson.

I have no doubt this particular guy was back more than once since my time. I still remember his name and what he looks like as well as the specific noteworthy line he wrote on that dentist clinic wall.

14

Visits

Heather came to visit me every chance she got. On one of her first visits, I asked her to get me a short-term subscription to the newspaper. Like the movie *Groundhog Day*, where the main character gets stuck in a time loop reliving the same day over and over, each day in prison seemed a repeat of the previous one. We left our cells at the same time, ate our three meals at the same time, went to work at the same jobs, mustered together and walked back to our cells like slaves wearing prison greens.

If not for the newspaper, I wouldn't have known whether it was Tuesday or Saturday. The only thing that changed other than the newspaper was the inmates as new ones arrived or old ones left. Every day felt like a month. I now had empathy for caged hens, let out of their tiny coop for a brief walk once a day, then back inside the rest of the time.

Visitors usually guarded their talk when they came to Pentridge, as they didn't know who could overhear them and what they would do with the information. A heavy blanket of oppression lay over the entire place. At least I could look forward to seeing my beautiful wife, which was more than a lot of inmates. To begin with, I could only get box visits, which meant Heather and I sat on either side of a see-through wall that had slits to allow conversation, just like in the movies.

After a few of those, we were allowed contact visits, which are more personalised. For instance, we could sit at a table together, holding hands. But to enjoy a contact visit, I had to undergo strip-searches on the way into the visit and on the way out, which are very personal and unpleasant. The purpose was to ensure we weren't trying to transfer anything out of the prison the wrong way or bring anything in the officers didn't know about.

On one contact visit before I understood the rules, I asked Heather to bring in my wedding ring as I felt undressed without it. Upon my return through the strip-search area, the prison officer blasted me for trying to bring in contraband.

"It's only a ring," I tried to explain.

"Nothing unregistered goes out on a visit!" he barked angrily. "And certainly nothing unregistered comes in from one!"

"Yes, boss," I responded meekly.

After the first fortnight, Heather brought me my small New Testament, which made an immediate difference. She could have brought it earlier, but since I really prized it, I wanted to make sure first that my belongings wouldn't be getting stolen by other inmates, like the Adidas. Within a fortnight I was comfortable enough not to worry about my own belongings, so Heather brought it to me.

I was happy to be reading Scripture again. I began reading the book of Acts, including the various chronicles of different disciples being arrested and thrown in prison and how they conducted themselves. As I read, I felt God's companionship more and more.

I also purchased a notepad and pen through the prison canteen and began keeping a diary in which I journaled every day of my incarceration. This included who I met, what I'd done during that day, and what I thought God was saying to me throughout the day. I found writing these journal entries very relaxing, which became the chronicles of this biography. My mind would wander to connecting thoughts of elsewhere and other people. Friends' faces would pop up in my mind, and I would smile as I thought of better days.

I often thought of my earlier days of surfing. I would close my eyes and be out in the water with mates, the wind and energy of the ocean propelling me along a wave. Those ruminations carried me back to a place I loved and a time when there was little to worry about. Then my daydreaming would be interrupted by a cellmate. "Feel like a brew, Niv?"

I'd open my eyes and smile. "Thanks, mate. White with one!"

During this time period, I met my first Prison Fellowship volunteer, who was doing his rounds of the different divisions. He came over while I was working in the kitchen and introduced himself. I'd never heard of Prison Fellowship at that stage and was highly suspicious of everyone. His greeting and questioning, gentle and friendly as it was, took me by surprise so that I didn't hear much of what he said, the questions in my head drowning out his voice. *Who is this bloke? What does he want?*

It seemed odd for the man to be walking freely around the prison. I assumed he must be from the government or a social worker or something like that. He asked me how I was handling prison and if I needed anything.

"Nah, I'm okay, mate!" I fobbed him off and walked away. I wish now I could have that time over again to make him feel more welcome, have a chat, and maybe meet him again on his rounds.

Walking back to our cells after work presented certain dilemmas. We were lined up single-file for the march back. As the long trail of inmates made their way to their cells, the prison officers would randomly beckon some of us one by one to leave the line and stand off to one side in a shorter parallel line. They would then search our bags for stolen goods or items that shouldn't be there. If they found anything other than our own kit, we'd get written up.

Sixteen hours is a long time without a snack, and of course those who worked in the kitchen had access to bread, butter, sauces, salads, and meat. So the fellas from our cell who worked in the kitchen started a sandwich-smuggling gauntlet, taking turns making sandwiches to eat later in the night over a TV show.

The trouble with that? It was officially illegal. On my first contraband run, I had two huge sandwiches tucked down deep at the bottom of my bag and wrapped in my tee-shirt. Half a sandwich each for the four of us.

As we arrived at this regular area of the journey, I started to sweat a little. I'd had nothing to hide up to this point, and it's amazing what a bit of guilt can do to your facial expressions. Then the guard looked straight at me and pointed his finger. Like the drug courier from the movie *Midnight Express*, it felt like he knew I was guilty.

I kept a straight face, but sweat beads were clearly forming on my forehead and top lip. My head felt like a flashing neon sign screaming, "Guilty!" Sure my game was up, I was just about to step over to the parallel line when the guard's finger suddenly changed direction to the guy behind me.

Phew! I told myself. *That was close!*

I kept my cool and managed to courier the sandwiches the rest of the way without incident. I gave my cellmates a wink as I entered the cell. As soon as the prison officers had locked the cell door and moved on, I transferred the sandwiches to their secret hiding place. This was a loose plywood corner flap on our cupboard, which we could peel back ever so slightly. Behind it was a hollow where we could hide our goodies. After the final muster for the night, we pulled out the sandwiches. In silence but with big smiles, we washed our snacks down with cups of coffee.

Pentridge had a make-shift gym on a lower level, which I used a few times. No stainless-steel Olympic-brand weight machines here. Just rusty old iron free-weights with very basic benches. On one side of the gym was a large barred window through which I could see K (Jika Jika) Division. Built in 1980 at a cost of AU$7 million to house Victoria's most notorious prisoners, it was laid out in weird modules connected by radiating spokes that looked to me like some intergalactic craft had landed in the centre of hell by mistake.

After working many days on the dishes, I was finally promoted to cutting carrots. I rejoiced, figuring I was now on my way to success. But that job had only lasted half a day when I was informed that I'd been called up for classification (classo). This meant I'd be receiving a more permanent housing assignment depending on how high-risk a prisoner I was, A and B being the most dangerous classifications. I was classified as C, the lowest risk level.

I was actually sorry to go as most of the guys had been good to work with. And they weren't happy about me leaving either. I was easy to get along with and worked hard, which they appreciated, as lazy guys like the one originally assigned with me to washing dishes made more work for everyone. Billy, an inmate doing a long stretch for armed robberies, was in charge of the kitchen. He came up to me personally as I was saying my goodbyes and shook my hand, wishing me all the best on my journey.

"Sorry to see you go, Niv. I've really appreciated your work, but I hope I don't see you back here in a hurry," he said with a wry grin.

"Thanks, mate, I've enjoyed my stay," I replied. "And don't worry. I like you guys, but you definitely won't be seeing me back here."

During my time washing dishes in that kitchen, God taught me five fruitful lessons He clearly thought I needed:

- Long-suffering.
- Forgiveness.
- To be content in whatever state I find myself.
- Not to despise the day of small things (Zechariah 4:10).
- Good things come to those who wait.

15

The Missing Kettle

Everywhere I walked within Pentridge Prison, there was a wall, fence, or locked gate. Every stone wall was topped by razor wire, making it hard not to feel like a sheep captured in a series of pens. Before prison, I'd spent most of my work life outdoors, so inside these walls I felt totally captive in both body and mind. I could understand why people try to escape.

My path through Pentridge was one of apprehension at every step. Nothing was familiar to me except my ability to get on with people. To get through a gate, I would yell as I approached, "Gate-up, Boss!" Upon which a prison officer would question me. If my story stood up, the guard would open the magnetic lock on the gate to let me through.

On one especially freezing-cold day, a group of other prisoners and I were escorted to A Division, which was considered one of the better divisions with more liberties than divisions for hard-core long-term prisoners. On our way there, we walked through enclosed wire walkways with a short stop at a hut, where we removed our clothes for a strip-search. The entire transfer took about two hours despite it being in the same prison.

Once we'd arrived in A Division, we were taken to the central circle where I was allotted Cell 50 in the middle tier of a three-tiered cell block. This was a small single cell with a single bed against one wall, a toilet at the end of the bed, and a TV. One missing item was any kind of electric kettle for boiling water to make tea or coffee.

Hot running water was also not provided in individual cells but was available down in the central circle. For a night-time cuppa prior to lock-up, I would fill my mug and a bright-yellow plastic tub provided for dishwashing with hot water, then race upstairs to my cell, hoping to get at least a second cup of hot tea or coffee before the water went cold. That first night, an inmate I'd met before in D Division gave me some butter so I could make toast and eat it cold later in my cell. But no one could help me with acquiring a kettle.

After breakfast the next morning, I played a game of pool with an older guy who used to box professionally, then was invited for a game of volleyball. After the games, I wrote letters, made phone calls to friends, introduced myself to other inmates, and spent time in the evening reading my Bible. Since I was new to A Division and had little in terms of canteen supplies, I approached the senior prison officer, asking if I could get some rations such as coffee, tea, and biscuits. He was helpful but couldn't get me a kettle.

The next day, I was rostered onto the horticultural gang. My feet were still red-raw and bleeding from my stint at dishwashing, and this outdoor job would mean wearing gumboots again. I approached the senior prison official and explained my problem. Apparently, raw, bleeding feet wasn't a good enough excuse, so off I went with the gang.

When we returned from work, security was searching the cells for drugs. They'd left my cell a mess. My feet were equally a mess, and when I peeled my bloodied socks off, skin came with them. They itched so badly every step drove me crazy. When I showered, I'd race in, scrub quickly while keeping my feet covered, then get out since no one wants a leper in the shower with them.

I was still trying to get my hands on a kettle for my cell. While approaching one guy who worked in the A Division store, I couldn't resist asking about something that didn't look quite right. "Hey, what happened to your calf muscle? It looks a bit mangled."

"Oh, that!" he responded. "It's a long story, but I'll give you the short version. I was at the six-year mark of an eight-year sentence when I got sick of jail and tried to escape. I slashed my calf on the razor wire when jumping off the bluestone wall. All the guards had to do was follow the blood trail. I made it less than half a kilometre before they caught me. That added another six years to my sentence, so I'm now doing fourteen total."

That's a pretty expensive price to pay! I thought, listening in amazement. I hadn't been in prison long enough to be that desperate, but I was already sick of the time I'd done and the future I was looking at. And I was looking at months, not years.

Though it felt like months, I was only in A Division for

a week. I'd been there a few days when a new group came through from D Division. One prisoner was a fresh-faced, innocent-looking young guy, visibly embarrassed and scared at his situation. As they lined up at the store to get their blankets and other supplies, Mangled Calf looked directly at the young kid and yelled out in a gruff voice, "OOOhh, HERE COMES MY NEW GIRLFRIEND!" He was joking, but the kid didn't know it and wet himself from fear.

During one contact visit from my wife and family while I was in A Division, I mistakenly used the wrong toilet. Instead of being separated by glass, visits here were in a large open area where inmates and visitors could sit at a table together and talk. Needing a toilet break, I inadvertently walked into the visitors' toilet instead of the one assigned to inmates. As the saying goes, all hell broke loose. Prison officers came from everywhere, batons out. Slamming me up against the wall, they immediately began a pat-down while yelling questions.

"What were you doing in there?"

"Put your hand up and face the wall!"

"Spread your legs! Spread 'em, I said!"

I parroted off the customary response. "Sorry boss! It won't happen again, boss!" I can understand how an inmate in the visitor's toilet with or without a visitor might be a security problem, but their reaction did seem excessive at the time.

Once locked in our cells each evening, there wasn't much to look forward to, so prisoners watched TV, read, wrote letters, or kept a diary. I read a lot of the Bible in this period while drinking my two night-time cups of tea or coffee.

Obviously, a kettle for hot water is an integral part of this survival system, and I wouldn't have thought it that impossible to get one.

Then one day thanks to my Mangled Calf friend at the store, I finally acquired a kettle. But that nightly pleasure proved even more short-lived than my good job in the kitchen. That very next afternoon, I learned I'd been reassigned to the Dhurringile prison farm.

As I mentioned, prison farms were where most low-level offenders were sent along with more serious criminals nearing the end of their sentence. During my Scripture readings over prior weeks, the message of "good works" kept popping up time and time again. As Christians, we are told to work as though for God, so others will see our good works and praise God (Matthew 5:16; Colossians 3:23-24). We are told that without evidencing our faith through good works, belief in God is meaningless since even Satan believes in God (James 2: 14-26). We are told that even as Christians we will be judged and rewarded according to our good works (Romans 2:6-10; 2 Corinthians 5:10; Galatians 6:9).

After a lifetime of not taking responsibility for my actions, it was clear God wanted to see responsibility from me. But it also appeared he wanted to see good works driven by faith. By sending this message through Scripture into this hellhole, he might have been giving me some idea of my immediate future—which was definitely about to involve a lot of hard work!

That afternoon, a number of us were ushered into the

rear of the "Dhurringile Express," the stainless-steel inmate delivery van bound for Dhurringile Prison Farm. The van was an air-conditioned box with no windows. We could hear the revving of the engine, and the van swayed from side to side as we rounded sharp bends. Occasionally, we lifted off our seats when the van hit a pothole.

The total drive to this custodial oasis near Shepparton, Victoria, took about two and a half hours. The first hour was uncomfortable as we were all strangers, just a bunch of different men brought together by the law. With prisoners, you don't know who's who or what some people will do with too much knowledge of you, so it's preferable to remain guarded. But after a while, we began chatting lightly amongst ourselves. We weren't close mates by the time we reached Dhurringile, but at least the frost had evaporated.

Dhurringile is an aboriginal name meaning "emu's back," so named for the shape of the original property and its many emus. It had originally been a huge pastoral estate running upwards of fifty thousand sheep, and its double-story towered brick mansion had more than sixty rooms along with outbuildings, staff quarters, its own gas works, and an entire village for estate workers. The Australian government had used it as an internment camp for German and Italian prisoners during World War Two. It was then purchased by the Presbyterian Church of Australia, which used it as a home and training farm for migrant boys.

In 1965, the government took it over and converted it into a prison farm. The once luxurious mansion now had steel bars on the windows and magnetically-locked doors. But the grounds with its circled driveway still boasted a well-kept front garden of multi-coloured roses and other flowering plants, tall gum trees, and a well-manicured lawn.

Since the van had no windows, our first view of the place was from the rear of the mansion where they delivered the new inmates. As a working farm, Dhurringile had no high bluestone walls topped with calf-slashing razor wire, just a normal wire fence and driveway gate that stood open. As we climbed out of the van, I could see orchards of fruit trees, a tennis court, and even a small, dirty swimming pool. Standing majestically against the backdrop of the mansion, was a large jacaranda tree, its blue-mauve flowers resplendent as the warm sun sprinkled its rays through the foliage. It looked so regal, the king of all the farm's trees.

Yeah! I told myself with sudden optimism. *I have a good feeling about this place!*

16

Room With a View

Once we'd unloaded from the van, a prison officer gave us our lodging assignments. "Neyland, you're in 8 Dorm at the top of the stairs to the left."

"Yes, boss." A bit more prison-savvy than when I'd arrived at D Division a month earlier, I grabbed my sack and ran to 8 Dorm, determined to get a good bed. Leaping up the stairs two at a time, I was first to reach the dorm room, which had two large windows overlooking the mansion's entrance.

I immediately grabbed a bed under a window. At Pentridge, I'd developed a smoker's cough due to inhaling cigarette smoke from other inmates. Here the window bars were far enough apart I figured I could raise the window a bit and suck some clean air. Unfortunately, my window position didn't help much since of the other six inmates sharing the room, five turned out to be smokers.

I'd made my bed and was settling in when I was summoned to the front desk to speak to the security prison officer. He asked, "Are you one of the Neylands from Patchewollock?"

It turned out the officer was originally from around

Patchewollock. I think he was hoping for someone familiar with his hometown. Thinking a moment, I answered what I assumed to be true. "No, boss, I'm from Sydenham."

A few years later while looking up my family history, I discovered that I actually was related to the Patchewollock Neylands through my grandfather, the original Niven Neyland, who had many brothers. He and six of those brothers fought in World War One, all returning alive. My grandfather was shot in the neck and captured in the 1915 August Offensive at Gallipoli, spending the next three and a half years in a Turkish prison camp. A plaque at a park in Donald, Victoria, displays most of the Neyland brothers' names.

The comparative freedom at Dhurringile was refreshing. Instead of Pentridge's 4:00 p.m. lock-up, here we were free to move around until 8:00 p.m. Those extra few hours made a big difference to the stress levels and anger of the inmates. One evening about a fortnight after I got there, I was walking around the mansion grounds. Suddenly, a burden I hadn't even realised I'd been carrying since my arrival at Pentridge lifted, and I actually felt peaceful.

Looking up at the night sky, I raised my hands to the heavens and said, "Thank you, Lord!"

Being a working farm, Dhurringile paid a lot of its own way by doing community work. After my feet issues working in gumboots at Pentridge, I felt I needed a more suitable job here. One inmate told me he could get me a job making seedling boxes. That sounded great, so I walked down to the farm supervisor's office to ask about a job. I'd totally forgotten the orientation we'd received on arrival. I was immediately sent back to the mansion, where two prison officers lectured me sternly as to exactly what I could and couldn't do, where I could and couldn't go, and the penalties attached to non-compliance.

Later that evening, I wandered down to a multi-purpose hall outside the main mansion called the Visit Centre. At the time, I didn't realise what a big part this large rectangular building would play in my life. Built on a lower level than the mansion, it had two entrance paths. Visitors used the northern path while inmates used the southern path. The central hall section was glass-paned on both sides so you could see right through the building.

As I was looking through the double set of glass panes to a paddock beyond the Visit Centre, I suddenly realised the time. *Oops! I'm going to be late for 8:00 p.m. muster!* Hurriedly, I rushed back to 8 Dorm to be checked off and locked in for the night.

Breakfast the next morning also proved quite different from Pentridge. For one, we had fresh milk from the farm's cows and pure honey from the beehives. I drank milk in my coffee and tea until the day I saw a prisoner plunge his plastic jug into the large stainless-steel bucket of fresh milk, his tattooed forearm disappearing into the creamy white cow's juice up to his elbow. I had no way of knowing whether the guy had hepatitis or some other disease or just bad personal hygiene. But for me, that was the last drop of milk I had for the rest of my sentence. From that day on, I had water on my Weetbix and porridge and drank black coffee.

One breakfast time, we were given a special treat of bacon and eggs. With eighty-odd inmates, you can imagine a hundred and sixty fried eggs dripping with oil in a large aluminium tray next to an equally large tray of bacon. Add freshly-browned toast and butter, and the meal sounds quite sumptuous. And it might have been without the final ingredient.

That particular day was already a scorcher by the time we gathered for our pre-breakfast muster, one of many musters through the day to ensure we hadn't "done a runner." As we stood in the open-air quadrangle waiting for our names to be called out, the familiar fragrance of cooked bacon wafted across the quadrangle, firing up our hunger pangs. When muster ended, we headed ravenously for the mess hall.

But once we entered, our excitement dissipated. The large trays of food looked as though they were carpeted with black peppercorns. But when we drew closer, the final ingredient revealed itself as countless black flies stood skating atop the oily eggs. We all looked at each other, dumbstruck, our hunger swiftly fading. But was the sight enough to put us off such a special feed?

All we needed was a leader, and here he came. Grabbing the wooden handle of the stainless-steel egg flipper, he announced, "Oh, well, let's not just stand here, boys!"

Flipping a few skating-rink eggs aside on his way to lower layers of clean ones, he dropped a couple on his plate. Then with a challenging smile, he handed the flipper to the next guy. "C'mon, you chicken, get into it!"

With an equally challenging smile, the second guy snatched up the flipper. "May as well. You only live once!"

I followed suit with two eggs and a couple of bacon rashers. My personal philosophy is that if you just add tomato sauce to food, all problems and distastes disappear. So I added sauce, and they did!

My first job at Dhurringile turned out to be hoeing lettuce—once again in gumboots! I applied to be assigned a different job, citing my feet issues. I guessed that could take some time, so when I spotted a notice for a free six-day computer course, I applied for it. I knew nothing about computers, but I figured it might be a useful course I could squeeze in with my job. That was the first of many courses I took while at Dhurringile.

Anxious to relieve my feet, I requested to see the prison doctor to get some ointment. I was informed with a shrug, "Bad luck. He's just been here and won't be back for a fortnight. You'll have to wait till then to see him."

What was it with prisons and fortnights? A few days later I woke up with the flu but was again told that I'd have to wait another nine days to see the doctor. By the time he finally did arrive, I was over the flu.

During this time, I'd been reading and meditating on the messages sent to the seven churches in the first three chapters of Revelation. I couldn't help wondering how could so many of them could get so completely out of favour with God.

In fact, that study impacted me so deeply that almost thirty years later I ended up writing a book on them. One passage especially struck from the message to the Church of Laodicea, where God rebukes them for their apathy and complacency.

> I know your works, that you are neither cold nor hot. I could wish you were cold or hot. So then, because you are lukewarm, and neither cold nor hot, I will vomit you out of My mouth. (Revelation 3:15-16)

As I read those verses, I thought back to the many times I'd been equally lukewarm in following God, the last time costing me and my family so much pain. I realised how easy it was to drift into complacent disobedience. In fact, each time I thought of the folly of those churches, my thoughts returned to my own foolishness. I came to understand that developing a plan to live in obedience to God is the easy part. Carrying it out each and every day is the tricky bit, as Scripture reminds us.

> Do not merely listen to the word, and so deceive yourselves. Do what it says. Anyone who listens to the word but does not do what it says is like someone who looks at his face in a mirror and, after looking at himself, goes away and immediately forgets what he looks like. (James 1:22-24).
>
> Therefore do not worry about tomorrow, for tomorrow will worry about itself. Each day has enough trouble of its own. Matthew 6:34

I've found a day to be a long time!

17

Church Comes to Prison

Despite all the challenges of living and working alone through her pregnancy, Heather was my most faithful visitor during my nine months at Dhurringile. She didn't miss a single visiting day of my entire sentence except for a couple of occasions when other plans interfered and when she gave birth to our son. Every Saturday and Sunday, she would drive up by herself or with various friends and relatives. That is faithfulness in anyone's language! I am so thankful to God that Heather is my wife. When I am with her, I am as rich as anybody can be in this life.

Contact visits at Dhurringile were three full hours, much longer than at Pentridge. We could cook a barbecue if the hot plates at Visit Centre were free, so Heather often brought goodies to prepare a simple feast.

On one weekend, another inmate smuggled some wrapped chicken fillets from the kitchen to cook for his family on one of the hot plates. As usual, prison officers asked, "Anything to declare?"

"No!" the inmate responded. The trouble was that he'd tucked the fillets down his pants, which now began slipping down his pant leg. A few of us could tell from his wriggling what was going on. As he shuffled into the Visit Centre, the prison officers kept their eyes on him. We could see them thinking, "He was walking just fine when he got here!"

Sitting down at a table with his family, the inmate waited until the officers had lost interest, then slid his hand down his pants to retrieve the fillets. He'd gotten away with it. But he later told us sheepishly that his wife had been furious.

"You're already in prison for taking risks!" she'd scolded him. "And now you're doing this!"

Speaking of risks, by this point Heather's "baby bump" really began to show, which made me feel so proud to be an expectant dad and husband. One weekend when she came for a visit, the prison officers were searching every vehicle looking for drugs, which can be difficult to control in this type of open prison. When Heather arrived in her elderly light-blue Datsun Bluebird, the head of security waved her on through without a vehicle check.

Driving through the checkpoint, she pointed to her cantaloupe-shaped stomach and announced, "I have a bomb in there!"

Thankfully, they just laughed. Nowadays, she'd never get by saying something like that as it would be taken seriously!

Interestingly, Dhurringile seemed to welcome visits from Christian ministry groups, clearly considering them a positive influence on the inmates. One lovely Christian couple, Tom and Wynne, would come periodically on Friday evenings. They'd play some music, deliver a short Christian message, and serve a spread of delicious food, which of course the prisoners couldn't resist!

A group called New Wine Ministries (NWM) was the prison's Christian influence on Sunday evenings. Headed up by Denys and Christine Parnell, they were a lovely group who would feature more in my life as time went on. They played guitars and sang worship music, taking requests from the inmates, then preached a short sermon. Always cheerful, their company was refreshing, and the number of inmates showing up to their meetings was no surprise.

Some inmates had been brought up in church before going astray and enjoyed the familiar hymns and preaching. Some liked the atmosphere of peace and love the team brought with them. Others just yearned for a better, normal life, and that weekly hour of worship seemed to represent this for them. Whatever our reasons, we were all attracted like bees to a honey pot and always enjoyed our time there.

One inmate who regularly attended was a man with a big, bushy beard. He went by the nickname of JC for the obvious reason that he looked like traditional pictures of Jesus Christ. I had a chat with him on his first visit to the NWM worship service. "G'day, mate. I'm Niv. What brings you to church?"

"Oh, I just like the music," he responded. "And it's good to see someone else other than inmates"

After that, we chatted occasionally at services. I eventually asked him, "Do other inmates ever give you a rough time for coming?"

His response was colourful but plain. "They may, but stuff

'em if they do! I'll do my jail the way I want, and they can do theirs the way they want!"

I found out that JC had attended church on the outside, so it wasn't unfamiliar territory. But prison had left him hardened and with a lot of difficult issues on his mind. We had many talks, both about his life issues and the power of Jesus Christ over all problems. I obtained a Gideons pocket New Testament for him and underlined numerous scriptures in it. I also wrote a nice inscription of hope.

Gideon's International is a ministry that for more than a century has been giving away Bibles and New Testaments, placing more than two billion copies in hotels, hospitals, prisons, schools, convalescent homes, domestic shelters, refugee camps, and far more in over two hundred countries. Thankfully, the Australian prison system is one place where they donate Bibles, so throughout my time there, I was able to obtain copies for prisoners who requested them.

During this time, I learned of another committed Christian in Dhurringile named Trevor. I didn't approach him immediately, just observed his behaviour. After all, plenty of people call themselves Christians but don't live a committed life. Take me, for instance, before the collision.

Little did I realise that Trevor was doing the same to me. Once we were satisfied with what we saw, we met for a coffee and ended up becoming good friends, remaining brothers in Christ today. Trevor had come to Christ through a Prison Fellowship volunteer in another prison years before. The crime for which he was in prison was one his new nature would never commit. Since becoming a Christian, he'd learned to look forward instead of back in regret, and his daily life matched his faith.

Meanwhile, I continued looking for a job that didn't involve gumboots and wet feet. One inmate told me to talk to the prison governor about a grass-cutting job he knew was about to become available. I did so, but the governor turned me down.

"You will need to apply for the job like everyone else," he told me. "Applying for a job helps inmates when they get out."

I'd already had plenty of job interview experience. But many inmates are unemployed when they come to prison, so I understood the governor's reasoning. The next day, I headed down to the seedling shed for my daily quota of hoeing lettuce. Calling me back, the security prison officer mentioned that a job was available washing vehicles and doing some gardening around the mansion.

"You can have the job if you want it," he said. "But you'll still need to formally apply first."

The job sounded better than grass-cutting, so I filled out the application. I wish every job I've gone for proved that easy to get! My responsibilities included washing the prison farm's few cars and a small bus as well as caring for a garden at the rear of the mansion. Owning a garden supplies and plant nursery had already given me a passion for gardening. Now I just had to develop a passion for washing vehicles, something I will admit I never mastered to the present day.

I was still reading my Bible any time I got the chance, especially on my bed once we were locked in for the night. One 8 Dorm roommate, Linc, was just nineteen years old but already had quite a few tattoos, including up the sides of his neck, and came from a tough neighbourhood much like Port Melbourne, the crime-ridden wharf-side district where I'd once worked.

"What are you reading?" he asked me one evening.

"The Bible." I lifted my copy so he could see it.

His expression showed interest. "I've never read it. What's it about?"

"Well, it's about life. The Bible gives us the story of our lives. It shows us when and how we were created. Who created us. The purpose of our life. And most importantly, what happens after we die."

"After we die?" he repeated, looking confused.

I could see he needed more information, "That's right, Linc. After all, we human beings are more than just a beating heart, brain, bones, and muscle. What is the one thing that makes you Linc? It's the spirit God has placed inside your physical body that gives you your personality and makes you a unique individual. If not for that spirit, we would be just a useless mass of flesh and bones. Those physical parts are not who we really are. That's why there's a saying when people die that they've 'given up the spirit.'"

I could see the fascination in his eyes, so I turned my Bible to the gospel account of Christ's death.

And when Jesus had cried out with a loud voice, He said,

"Father, into Your hands I commit My spirit." Having said this, He breathed His last. (Luke 23:46)

"We see here that Jesus understood it wasn't his physical body that gave him life but his spirit," I explained, "After Jesus died, his physical body was still hanging there on the cross. But his spirit had gone to his Father in heaven the moment he gave his last breath."

Linc seemed to get that explanation. I went on to explain how all of humanity from Adam and Eve onward had been separated from God because of sin (Romans 3:23) and how Jesus had come to give his life in sacrifice on the cross to pay the penalty for our sins (John 3:16).

"If we repent of our sins, place our faith in Jesus, and confess Jesus as Saviour and Lord, He not only restores us to a relationship with God, but our spirits will live eternally with God in heaven. If we reject God's free gift of salvation through Jesus, our spirits are bound for hell. That's why it's so important to understand what happens after we die. Too many people don't realise they're bound for hell because they rarely think of what goes on after death."

Linc was clearly starting to get it. Despite the many tattoos and often-rough language, he was basically a good kid, and I came to really enjoy his company. While our other roommate played cards, smoked, and made cigarette cases out of matches, Linc and I ended up sitting together on my bed night after night, reading the Bible and discussing different topics. When he asked me what being a born-again Christian was like, I shared the changes the Holy Spirit had made in my life and how I awoke each morning with a feeling of joy and peace despite being in prison.

One evening after we'd finished one such session, he rang up his girlfriend and told her jokingly, "I think I'm becoming a born-again Christian."

Linc was released before I witnessed him make a commitment to Jesus Christ. But the gospel seed was sown in very fertile soil, and I continue to pray that at some point since he has indeed made a profession of faith and that I will one day see him again in heaven.

18

Had Enough, Time for Change!

Once Linc was released, the blasphemy and swearing in 8 Dorm really got to me. In my prayer time, I asked God how Joseph in the book of Genesis managed to keep himself pure despite the disagreeable things going on around him, including his brothers selling him into slavery, a master's wife trying to seduce him, and ending up in prison for a crime he didn't commit (Genesis 37–50).

My frustration really boiled over as I was reading in the apostle Peter's second epistle about the Old Testament patriarch Lot and how troubled his soul had been due to the evil actions and language of his neighbours.

> He [God] rescued Lot, a righteous man, who was distressed by the depraved conduct of the lawless, for that righteous man, living among them day after day, was tormented in his righteous soul by the lawless deeds he saw and heard. (2 Peter 2: 7–8)

I wrestled with whether I should stay in 8 Dorm as a witness for the gospel or pray that God would get me moved somewhere else. I wasn't sure what God wanted me to do, but within myself, I felt I'd had enough. Like Lot, my soul felt troubled every time I was locked in that room with those guys. I prayed a simple and to-the-point prayer. "Lord, my soul is troubled. Please move me from here!"

Astonishingly, the very next morning a prison officer came up to me and asked without any prompting, "Hey, Neyland, how'd you like a dorm change?"

I didn't bother asking which dorm, who I'd be rooming with, or whether I'd have a window bed. I just responded with enthusiasm, "Absolutely, Boss!"

"Okay, grab your things and head down to 12 Dorm," the officer told me. "Your bed should be clear by now."

Grabbing my bag and Bible, I headed down to 12 Dorm. At the far end of a long corridor, the room had one middle window with the usual vertical rust-coloured steel bars. More importantly, it had only two other people along with a large fish tank. What an immediate answer to prayer! Another blessing was that only one of my new roommates Larry, was a smoker and not a constant one, just the occasional roll-your-own with a coffee.

The fish tank belonged to Larry. He'd been in for about fifteen years and was a GP (Governor's Pleasure), which meant that the State Governor, acting on advice from Government, chose when he'd be released back into society as opposed to a typical sentence where the minimum and maximum penalties were set by the court. The prison had allowed him to keep a fish tank, and he'd caught some small fish from the prison farm pond to stock it.

Larry was a quiet bloke and peaceful to be around, interested only in his fish. My bed was next to the fish tank, so in the evenings after lock-up, I could lie on my side and watch the fish. It was a really calming experience.

There was another advantage to having Larry as a roommate. He was a master at getting knots out of your back or loosening twisted muscles. I don't know where he learned it, but he helped quite a few of us who had trouble. One inmate woke up at midnight with muscle spasms after a gruelling leg workout in the gym. A blood-curdling cry from his dorm penetrated the barred windows as if someone had been stabbed. First Aid officers could do nothing for him. Eventually, Larry was called, and after fifteen minutes of intense and careful massage had the muscles loosened and back in their rightful places. From that instance, Larry's reputation for muscle magic reached new heights.

Notwithstanding his massaging talents, Larry's case was a sad one. He seemed to live a lonely life. One weekend, he had a visit scheduled. He'd gotten a haircut in preparation, which cost him a packet of smokes. That morning, he was out of bed early, showered, shaved, and as well-dressed as any inmate in green clothing could be. He looked quite presentable and was excited to meet his visitors.

All during my own three-hour visit with my wife, I never caught sight of Larry in the Visit Centre. I feared the worst—that his visitors had changed their minds. Sadly, I was right. When I returned to 12 Dorm, Larry was lying on his bed reading a book about fish. He looked as though he'd been crying, something you don't admit to in prison.

I bought him a can of Coke, a small and useless soother for his loneliness and feeling of being unwanted. From there, I asked, "Larry, would you like to come out with me when my wife visits next? We'd love to have you."

"Yes, thanks!" he responded with deep emotion. It was a pitiful way to exist. Larry was a good bloke and deserved more. We became friends.

My other roommate went by the nickname of Kaktes (cactus). Of Croatian heritage, he was about 1.88cm tall (6'2"), tanned, muscular, with longish black hair who looked like he belonged to some tribal royalty. Though smiling and cheerful, Kaktes didn't suffer idiots easily. But the three of us got on well. Kaktes suggested we take turns on weekends to make sure Larry had someone to visit with him. It was a good call.

But despite new friendships and the camaraderie they brought, I missed my wife enormously. This is possibly the most distressing negative about prison. Besides stripping us of our dignity, which we can only surrender if we choose to, it renders us lonely for the entire sentence. Inmates are not alone in prison, but most are continuously lonely. You miss the intimacy of conversation and mingling with those you know well and who know you well. There is nothing like family and friends to make you feel human.

The further we get as a society from God's teachings, the more prisons we end up having to build and the more money society must needlessly spend to maintain them. With prison, we have a system where the taxpayer pays most of the costs. They pay to incarcerate inmates. They pay again when inmates are released and can't find a job due to their incarceration. They pay if the ex-inmate has been damaged by institutionalisation. The perpetrator pays, but the rest of society pays also. It is far from an ideal system and certainly expensive for the community.

And it all starts with sin. With deliberately choosing to disobey God's teaching. Take just one instance. For whatever reason, a small-time criminal burgles a few houses. Here are just some of the costly consequences to society:

- House owner pays in higher insurance costs and a new security system.
- House owner must repurchase stolen items.
- Society pays for prison-time of the new inmate at approximately $110,000 annually.
- Society pays for all medical expenses and educational courses undertaken by the inmate.
- Society pays for social security money upon release.
- Society pays for the parole officer's time for the period of parole.
- Society pays for the inmate's training courses to help get a job following release.

- More than fifty percent of inmates return to prison, and society pays all the above over again.
- Prison-time develops links to other criminals, if that is the inmate's nature, expanding the criminal network.
- And so on.

There are numerous reasons why people go to prison. It isn't as cut and dried as someone doing the wrong thing and paying the penalty. Many inmates are brought up without suitable role models. Whether men or women, we all need positive people in our lives who model for us what society needs us to become. The Bible provides us with the best depiction of what a role model should look like in the life of Jesus Christ.

Author and Pastor J.R. Miller wrote, "The only thing that walks back from the tomb with the mourners and refuses to be buried is the character of a man."

What this means is that we are known by our character, so it is in our best interest to develop our character to a suitable standard. Herein lies a problem. Unless taught, many inmates don't understand character development or the need for it. They have very few examples within their social circles that fit community expectations.

Furthermore, there is a vast chasm between knowing what to do and actually doing it. We all have trouble with that! I think determination is the bridge that crosses that chasm. Many inmates have to be taught how to build determination if they are to live life effectively outside prison without throwing in the towel when the going gets tough. Life isn't easy for many of them, in or out of prison.

Neither of my two new roommates had any issues with me studying my Bible. In fact, they both had a lot of questions. They wanted to verify the many stories they'd heard through the years about faith, love, heaven, hell, forgiveness, and a myriad of other topics. After evening lock-up, we'd make a brew of coffee or tea and sit around talking about God. Oddly, in prison, it isn't a taboo subject like it often is on the outside.

I eventually asked Heather to bring in my concordance and other study tools. With those, the answers got deeper with more biblical support. They say women can talk when they get together, but I think men can outdo them given the right day. We'd start on one subject. Three coffees and two hours later, we'd have gone through several of life's other topics, not always coming to a resolution but enjoying the discussions nevertheless.

Every weekend was special for me, and that had a lot to do with my wife. Most times, we'd enjoy a great lunch, and many times I had her all to myself. Despite the mass of people in the large, echoing Visit Centre, we felt as though we were completely alone and private.

But once Heather was gone, I missed her agonisingly. I'd lie on my bed and hug my pillow, imagining it was her. During our sparse visits, we'd see some other couples arguing loudly, the wife decrying that she'd bothered taking hours out of her day to come at all. In contrast, I recorded in my diary every precious moment I got to share with Heather.

I also recorded the name of every person who visited me during my incarceration. And I saved every letter I received while inside. I never want to forget those who supported Heather and me during that time whether our friendships drifted apart later in life or not. They were there for us in a time of great need, and for that, we will always be very appreciative.

On our visits, Heather and I would talk and talk, mainly about her pregnancy, how she was handling everything on the outside, and the future of our child once he or she was born. We'd kiss, hold hands, nibble the goodies she'd brought, and just be in love. Then the weekend would be over and Monday morning would arrive with another five days before we'd see each other again.

But at least we could talk to each other by phone. I could talk to Heather twenty-four hours a day and never tire of it. In between phone calls, Heather would write me letters. One time when I called, she was crying. She then revealed that she often cried while writing to me as it drove home all we were going through and the reality of how long we were to be separated. I cringed at her admission, knowing it was me who'd inflicted this pain on her. Clearly, there was more than one person doing my prison sentence!

One of those extra sentences for both of us was the fact that I was missing so much of Heather's pregnancy. The ultrasounds. Going to prenatal classes. The typical excitement of preparing a nursery. I missed walking down the street with my pregnant wife as proud as I could be. I missed it all. We missed it all.

But one thing we'd learned this far in our short marriage and spiritual walk as a couple was not to focus on what we'd missed but rather on how we'd been enriched. And that included Heather's pregnancy, as it gave Heather to have something—someone—other than me and prison to concentrate on.

I believed then and believe now that our son Niv Neyland, Jr. was a timely blessing sent by God just when in His perfect wisdom and foreknowledge God knew we most needed it. We were never able to have any other children, so our son's birth in such difficult circumstances became even more special.

19

Living in the Here and Now

One day, Larry made a new fish tank and brought it into our dorm. We celebrated with a coffee as we helped him transfer the fish to their new home. I was pleased it didn't leak, considering how close it was to my pillow. Watching the tank that night, I wished I were a fish, just swimming around, being fed, never knowing about life's tragedies, never worrying about tomorrow, never setting up for the future. Everything with a fish is in the here and now.

I think I used to be like that in my teens. I'd hitchhike most places I went. When I did, I felt as free as a bird. I liked the fact that I never knew who'd pick me up. The conversations were always different, and I always had confidence I could get out of the vehicle when I wanted to. As we get older, we drop that casual side of life. But I think some of that living in the here and now might be worth hanging onto.

The next day, I yelled at a new young inmate who was trying to make people think he was a tough guy by kicking the timber bannister railing off the external staircase. It was clearly his first time inside, and someone must have told him he had to seem intimidating if he was to make it through.

Hearing me shout, he held up a dinner knife that for some reason he was holding in his hand. He started looking back and forth from the knife to me, then finally yelled some unintelligible grunt and walked away.

At least it took his mind off the bannister. After all, this was our home, and the rest of us didn't appreciate some new kid vandalizing it. That night at dinner, he walked up to my table with the same dinner knife in hand. Reaching across the table, he dug the knife into our butter cube and took it with him.

He clearly thought this was some kind of major threat. But as we watched him walk away, butter cube dangling from his knife, we burst into laughter. Those particular table companions were doing twenty-four years, thirteen years, and ten years respectively for murder.

A few nights later, he lined up with everyone else for the evening meal. When he reached the kitchen serving window where plates of food were handed out, he picked up his plate, then yelled for all to hear, "What's this crap?"

With that, he threw the plate of food back down on the counter. Unfortunately for him, we had a great new cook who was also an ex-boxer and didn't take kindly to that language. Leaning his heavily-built bulk across the counter, he demanded, "What did you say?"

The kid was stupid enough to repeat what he'd said. Removing his chef's apron as he went, the cook raced around to the door separating the kitchen and mess-hall and threw it open. Walking up to the loud-mouth, he gave the kid half a dozen classic fast punches, leaving his face a bloodied mess.

The prison officers overseeing the area didn't get there in time to stop the short-lived fray. But I think were satisfied justice had clearly been done. The very next morning, the kid was shanghaied to a real walled prison for making trouble, where he undoubtedly wished desperately he was back in the comforts of a prison farm. Prison officers like peace as much as prisoners, and the last thing any of us needed was a punk too cocky for his own good creating a nuisance.

Melbourne Cup Day, which is Australia's biggest horse race and a holiday, came around, a beautiful, sunny day. That evening, Larry came back from a living-skills outing, something long-term inmates are permitted to help in their assimilation with the outside world. He brought back some lamingtons, snowballs, and liquorice. While we didn't manage to pick the Cup winner, we enjoyed madly eating the goodies.

The next day, I began working on the rear garden beds. Jonesy, the senior officer, was pleased as this was his area. I worked hard pulling dead leaves from the lilies, severely pruning a tree, and did other tasks. I loved these days when I could work by myself. I would pray, praise the Lord, and sing songs to myself. The quiet was peaceful, and I enjoyed breathing the crisp spring air. If this weren't a prison, it would be a lovely place to visit.

Still, even good country air couldn't compare to sea air and the tang of salt water in your nostrils, something I was really missing, a reminder of how long it had been since I'd been out on the ocean in a sailing yacht and how much longer it would be. On one of our phone calls, I asked Heather to bring me some framed photos of yachts on her next visit. It wasn't just the clean smells and wind on my face, but the freedom of sailing that I really missed. No noisy motors, just the peace of the breeze on your face, a rain jacket, and the sails being trimmed to get more speed.

The mechanics of sailing has always intrigued me. The way the breeze soars through the sails, filling them up as if God himself had breathed on them. It astounds me how pulling a rope in here and there will fill the concave sails out till every square centimetre is being used to pick up more wind. With a good racing crew, nothing is wasted.

The following Sunday, a new visitor came in with New Wine Ministries. After I'd told him my name was Niven and that I lived in Melbourne, he asked if my surname was Neyland. It turned out that years back his family used to travel to Sydenham, Victoria, to the house church meetings run by my dad. He'd recognized the name Niven Neyland because that was also Dad's name. He told me how those meetings had planted Christ firmly in his heart. It was nice to hear Dad being acknowledged with such esteem.

Around this time, one of the prison farm inmates did a runner. The authorities didn't catch him for five weeks. The rest of us all watched the nightly news to see the next step in his escapade. It is easy but foolish to do a runner from a prison farm. You *will* get caught, and you won't get a second chance but will do the rest of your prison time behind high razor-topped walls.

Some weeks after the runner was recaptured, I knocked on the door next to our room, which was 14 Dorm. I was after a sewing needle I'd loaned them a couple of days earlier. When they didn't answer, I walked straight in. I almost choked on all the dope smoke.

It wasn't my place to rat on them. But on a similar note, two farm inmates got caught at a Shepparton nightclub by the drug squad. They were living in the more independent outside units where muster wasn't until 10:30 p.m. and there was no night-time lock-in. After dark, they would sneak across the farm grounds to where two girlfriends were waiting for them in a sports car with a change of clothing. Once out of their prison attire, they'd head to the nightclubs to ply their trade of buying and selling drugs.

As the saying goes, it's only a matter of time before your deeds catch up to you. Eventually, they missed getting back for the 10:30 p.m. muster, and the hunt was on. Once the drug squad picked them up, they were taken directly to a walled prison.

For the rest of us, it was good riddance. Inmates who exploit the farm because it has no walls make life very difficult for everyone else. The occasional small bending of the rules does no real harm but are perks such as every workplace has. Big, flagrant breaking of the rules will not only get you caught but make all the other inmates pay a penalty of losing privileges.

Kaktes had to go into Melbourne for a court case. When he returned, he brought with him a Gideon's Bible he'd started reading there to keep him calm. He couldn't stop telling me about the wisdom he'd discovered in the Old Testament book of Proverbs.

He returned just as Larry left 12 Dorm for an outside unit. This meant Larry was no longer locked in. It also meant Kaktes and I got a new roommate named Mick. About my age, Mick had a lovely girlfriend who was expecting their first child. His tangling with the law had been spur-of-the-moment and something he clearly regretted. Now he was keen on settling down and starting a family.

Mick proved eager to learn about God and the Bible, so Kaktes, Mick, and I ended up having Bible studies that went on until late into the night. There we were, three convicted criminals sitting on our beds discussing God in the heart of a prison. It doesn't get any better than that!

After a while, other inmates began joining our discussions, so I ended up having to move the Bible studies to the Visit Centre. I approached the prison's second-in-command with my request to hold them between Monday's and Friday's. He replied, "No worries. That's what it's for!"

With a larger group now participating, I added more structure. I started with a brief summary of biblical history from the creation and fall of Adam and Eve, the rise and fall of the nation of Israel, the life, death, and resurrection of Jesus Christ, the establishment of God's Church, all the way to end time events prophesied in the Book of Revelation. I focussed on repentance and salvation in every era as well as what the future might be like before the world ends. Most participants were astounded at the brutality of some of the battles described in Scripture as well as the compassion and mercy of God.

"When I see how much mercy God showed the Israelites, it gives me hope I'm not a lost cause after all," Mick told me one day. "I like the instruction God gave them. If only they'd obeyed! I get now where God was coming from as I wouldn't be in prison now if I'd just followed the instructions given to me."

Like Kaktes, Mick was fascinated by Scripture. I'd continued getting Gideons Bibles for those who wanted them, in which I always marked key passages that would help them get a good start on understanding God's word. When Mick got his copy, he started reading it at 8:00 p.m. and didn't put it down until 11:00 p.m.

Not long after, Mick received notice he was being released. The three of us got up early and had a final time of prayer together before the doors unlocked. Kaktes and I were sorry to lose him as a roommate but glad to see him on the outside. He was excited to actually attend church. He'd even asked his pregnant girlfriend if she'd go with him, and she'd said yes. God's Word never returns void (Isaiah 55:11), so I am trusting that Mick continued seeking out the truth of Scripture once he left.

Those Bible studies were important occasions for the farm inmates who attended. I would choose specific biblical eras to give them a grounding in God's history with humankind and how in every era people on the whole have ignored God and broken His laws. I likened this to our own situation confined in a prison filled with people who've heard of Jesus Christ but of whom few have chosen to follow Him. We also spoke of how Jesus is our only way to salvation and our only bridge back to God (John 14:6).

The Visit Centre Bible studies always led to lots of questions and discussions. This then seemed to generate further questions and discussions back in the dorms at night. God was indeed making a difference in many lives.

20

In God's Hands

Back before my court hearing, the senior investigating constable had let slip at one of my police interviews that John's ex-wife had been in contact with him about me. Tampering with a case in which you have a personal conflict of interest would be illegal for any police officer. But I had a strong suspicion my former sister-in-law would try to meddle.

Even with those suspicions, I'd been astonished at the severity of the original summons, which included sixteen charges. This same investigator had made clear that if I pleaded guilty to the main two charges, the other fourteen would be dropped. I'd done just that, which were the two charges for which I'd been sentenced.

But just five months into my sentence, I received a further summons from the senior investigating constable in the form of an Intention to Proceed letter, which informed me he'd now be pursuing the other fourteen charges. From my perspective, the letter confirmed my suspicions of meddling from John's ex-wife. I immediately rang the investigator, who refused to answer my direct questions about her involvement.

I then rang my solicitor. Not the alcoholic lawyer who'd lost me our garden supplies business but the competent one who'd handled my court case. He quickly sorted out the problem. It was clear the investigator's threats were hollow, and no new charges ended up being filed. Nor were there any further court appearances.

But during the time between receiving the Intention to Proceed letter and contacting my solicitor, I had a horrific nightmare that proved quite prophetic. I dreamed that my brother's ex-wife and her de facto "husband" had sold the business from under me and I wasn't able to do anything about it.

I awoke in a cold sweat with my heart racing. I didn't tell Heather of my nightmare as I didn't want to upset her further during her pregnancy. Like everything else since coming to prison, I knew I had to just leave it in God's hands.

But not long after, that nightmare played itself out in reality. My ex-sister-in-law and her common-law husband had already removed me as director. Now they went on to change the name of the business without my consent and completely removed me as a one-third shareholder. The business, accounts and the legal papers were now in their name.

It was the final blow. All the cash I'd poured into the business. The tough times working with my brother through a recession with massive interest rates. The hard work of building the business and revenues to an all-time high. All of this was now gone in a most underhanded manner.

"Look, Niven," my legal counsel told me, "With the current recession, high bank loan interest rates, and no current profits, it would cost too much to fight it. You might just need to walk away!"

I'd already walked away once when my ex-sister-in-law had shown up with a pair of bolt-cutters, called me a thief, and employed a squad of her police pals to throw me out of my own business. Being a cup-half-full sort of guy, I'd hoped this injustice would eventually be reversed. Now I was being told to walk away again?

If I'd hoped my lawyer was kidding, he wasn't! I received various offers from certain other inmates to assert some rough justice of their own on my behalf once they were released. I turned them down, of course, as I had no interest in breaking the law on my end.

During all of this, one other mind-boggling situation arose with my ex-sister-in-law. However unlikely, she had exactly the same name as my wife, at least their married names. The same first name, and the same last name. Even their middle names had only one letter difference. Easily confused. To top it off, their birthdays are April 25th and 26th respectively.

I'd already been transferred to Dhurringile when Heather was finally able to collect her "stolen" engagement ring from Broadmeadows Police Station. Her next appointment that same day was at the TAC (Traffic Accident Commission) in Melbourne to pick up $5000 for funeral reimbursements.

When Heather gave her name at the front desk, the receptionist responded, "Oh, you're here for the $250,000."

"No, only $5000," my wife clarified.

The woman immediately invited her back to her office to clear up the confusion. That was how Heather found out my ex-sister-in-law had claimed $250,000 in benefits (nearly $500,000 in 2021 equivalence) as John's grieving widow. She'd made it appear as though they'd never been separated and were residing together at the time of his death. Once Heather told them the actual situation, the TAC immediately stopped payment on the $250,000.

They then drove up to Dhurringile and got a further statement from me. They were astounded to learn that I was the one actually living with my brother in his house at the time of the collision and with Heather there for an additional four months after we were married. That ended my ex-sister-in-law's claim unless she tried to take TAC itself to court, which wasn't going to happen. You can imagine Heather and I were even less popular with her!

During this same time period, we'd been discussing the option of my wife moving to Shepparton to be close to the prison farm. Heather was reluctant since she'd already moved once to Melbourne, leaving her immediate family behind. Now that she'd developed strong relationships with my family, she didn't want to move again to Shepparton, where she'd have no one at all. She needed people she could visit and who could visit her during this time of isolation, especially with her pregnancy.

We were both praying about it, but the very thought of such an overwhelming decision on top of everything else brought Heather to tears. Then one Sunday afternoon, she met Christine Parnell from New Wine Ministries in the prison carpark. Christine knew who Heather was, so she'd approached to introduce herself. Heather thought this was friendly of her but a bit strange since she'd never met Christine before.

That evening after the NWM church service at Dhurringile, I called Heather to tell her I'd shared our predicament with Denys and Christine Parnell and that they had a proposition. I had no idea God was already working in the background and that Heather had actually met Christine that very afternoon.

Though the Parnells lived in Mooroopna, a small community divided from Shepparton by a river and bridge, Christine was actually from the United States. They would soon be traveling there for a six-week visit to see her family. Since this would leave their house empty, they wanted to offer it to Heather for the duration rent free.

The gesture was such a generous one we could hardly believe it. Heather moved up as soon as the Parnells flew out. Prison visits became much more manageable with a fifteen minute drive each way instead of two and a half hours, and Heather loved being back in a small country town.

Around this time, I began a plan to improve the back garden area for which I was responsible. The garden bordering the circle driveway in front of the mansion received top priority since this was what visitors saw, not to mention the prison governor and other officers when they looked out their office windows. Enthusiastically cared for by an inmate who seemed to know his stuff, it was laid out magnificently with beautiful roses of various colours and types, purple, pink, and lavender asters, and other ornamental plants and flowers.

Some brave inmates would try to steal a rose from the front garden as a gift for their wife or girlfriend when they visited. Stealing from the front garden came with penalties, so like chicken fillets down your pants, finding ways to get a rose while not getting caught was a constant game of chance. In stark contrast, no one bothered trying to steal flowers from the far more extensive rear gardens, which consisted of ordinary canna lilies and other cheap, stringy plants, barely watered.

As the rear gardener, I requested management for funds to purchase some decent plants that better suited the mansion. I was allotted $200, a mere start to buy plants for such a large garden. Another inmate suggested I write to local nurseries and ask them to donate some of their old stock. He'd done this at another prison, and it worked.

It was a good idea, so I approached the senior officer and got approval. From there, I drafted a few copies of a letter and sent them out to several local nurseries around the Greater Shepparton area. I was excited to receive positive responses from all of them. I ended up getting approximately $4000 worth of plants (about $12,000 today), including fifty rose bushes in large pots. The only catch was that we'd have to pick them up.

This was sorted out when the prison governor assigned an officer named Gary to take me and collect them in the prison bus. I don't think anyone was prepared for the number of plants coming back into the prison. On each bus trip, we returned with plants hanging out of windows, sitting on every seat, and filling the floor spaces.

By this time, Heather had moved to Shepparton. This was fantastic because it gave her so much more time and rest without all the driving. But the reality gripped me that I was still in prison and couldn't see her until the weekend, regardless of how much closer she lived.

On one beautiful, sunny bus trip with Gary to the nurseries, I recall looking out the window and thinking, *Wouldn't it be great to see my wife right now?* I went on to pray a silent, simple, and quite foolish prayer considering we were travelling on a road heading away from Shepparton, *Dear Lord, please let me see Heather today!*

Suddenly as though instructed by God, Gary spoke up. "I've got to go into Shepparton to get some things."

We immediately deviated into Shepparton, driving up and down a few streets to end up parking in front of the local Kmart. We both entered the store together since he couldn't let me out of his sight. Amazingly, Heather walked through the very same door less than a minute later. She'd been shopping next-door and felt a sudden urge to shop at Kmart.

What were the odds of all the stores in Shepparton she could have visited that day or times to shop?

Spotting Gary and me, Heather came up and planted a kiss on both our cheeks. Bending the rules, Gary told us, "You two sit on the park bench outside and have a talk while I finish the shopping."

When you only see your sweetheart twice per week, even twenty minutes on a public park bench in front of Kmart is special. It was such an incredible direct answer to prayer! Praise God for His mercy. He'd seen our two grieving hearts separated by my folly and in His great love had brought us together for that short time.

Thankfully, I'd earned a reputation by now as a trustworthy inmate, so Gary wasn't worried I'd run away. When he emerged from the store, I kissed my sweetheart and said, "See you on Saturday. I love you!"

Her reply was one we used often from a children's book about bears that was a favourite of Heather's. She loves cuddly bears. "I love you to the moon and back!"

Then Heather continued her shopping, and Gary and I proceeded on our journey to pick up plants and ferry them back to the prison.

21

Planting and Watering

Not long after that, the prison governor spoke to me civilly for the first time since I'd arrived in Dhurringile. I think he just got sick of inmates who called themselves Christians and didn't live up to it. And if he'd seen me a couple of years ago, he'd have been right!

He informed me the Minister of Corrections was due in a few days, and he wanted the grounds to look presentable for the visit. Especially since there'd be plenty of press showing up as well. The visit was important as it could mean more funding for the prison.

I understood wanting the place as nice as possible for the minister and press, so I got plenty of my new plants and planted them around the prison, trying to make it look like they'd been there for years. It worked. The entire place looked magnificent compared to the old shabby rear garden of a few months ago. The press added the gardens to the photo shoot, and the minister was delighted with what he saw.

After visiting the prison, the minister wanted to see some of the public projects the prison was involved in. One of these was Swim/Gym for debilitated people in a local nursing home. Many had suffered strokes or heart attacks and lost the use of limbs or brain function. During the week, a few trusted inmates, including myself, would bus into a community pool in Shepparton, where we would receive the nursing home patients, place them in a tyre or other floating device, and move them around so their muscles got some exercise.

Talking with them was difficult and sometimes impossible as some couldn't speak at all. On the day of the minister's visit, I'd completed my gardening and was part of the group helping with Swim/Gym. I'd been assigned to work with a man named Stan, who must have been around eighty years old. Incapacitated due to a stroke, he could only mumble words intelligible to himself alone. Stan and I were doing laps around the pool when the minister and his team arrived, me walking in the water with Stan afloat in the rubber tube.

The press seized the opportunity to snap a photo of Stan and me with the minister. There we were, the three of us, poles apart in many ways, doing our respective jobs for the community. The photo ended up in the newspaper. I was famous within the prison for a very short time, and the minister received good publicity. Sadly, Stan remained utterly unaware.

Gary and I continued to ferry plants in from the nurseries. But storing and watering them became two monstrous problems for me. We're talking $12,000 worth of plants in today's money, and there was still a lot of preparation work necessary to plant the bulk of them. By now I had plants stored in sheds, under the prison officers mess, down a deep well next to the mansion, under the Visit Centre, and any other place I could find where I could keep them alive, out of the full sun, and under lock and key.

This was now full summer, and the plants were drying out. Which meant I had to crawl down into some of those places with a hose to keep them watered until I could plant them. At this point, I had keys for so many locks in the prison that one officer told me, "Neyland, you have more keys to this prison than I do!"

The plants under the officers' mess were the most difficult to water. This caused me to spend much time under there. I could hear their voices filtering down through the floorboards while I watered and picked up a lot of information I shouldn't have. I could have sold that particular key for big money and had to keep it well-hidden when I wasn't using it.

The second-in-command to the prison governor had an inmate assigned to attend his garden much like my own assignment for the rear of the mansion. This inmate was little more than a cheap thief and would steal anything not bolted down if it made him look good to his direct boss. He stole the front gardener's new secateurs, my rake, and many of the plants I'd brought into the facility, even digging some out of my garden beds after I'd planted them.

I had some especially lovely plants hidden in the bottom of the unused well beside the mansion, which had no locks. One night, I received word this guy had found my stash and was at the well at this very moment. I headed over to see what was going on. Sure enough, he was climbing out of the well with some really nice plants and handing them to the big ex-boxer cook accompanying him. With a sneer, he told me to get lost.

Actually, the words were far stronger than that and not repeatable. There was little I could do. If I started a fight, I'd lose in two ways. Spiritual loss was a certainty as my peace would have gone immediately. I would have lost physically as well.

Either way, getting into a fight would be a poor testimony as a Christian, so I reluctantly walked away. I felt defeated doing so, but keeping the peace and a spiritual frame of mind was better in the long run than throwing it all away over a scuffle and a few plants. I'd have given the man some plants if he'd asked. I'd even have helped him pick which ones might go best in his garden. He didn't need to steal. It was just his nature.

I needed to get more of the plants into the ground as quickly as possible. Around this time, my job assignment changed from rear gardener and vehicle washer to the Visit Centre. This meant that I was now in charge of upkeeping both the inside facilities—cleaning floors, tables, toilets, windows, etc.—and the grounds associated with the Visit Centre.

The Visit Centre was the main part of the prison farm that family members actually saw. They came through the front gate and into a guard hut, where their belongings were searched for any possible contraband. From there, a short, narrow concrete path led downhill to their entrance into the Visit Centre. For wives, girlfriends, and older children especially, this is a walk of shame and embarrassment.

I had a vision to change that by transforming the Visit Centre landscaping. First, I established a long row of lovely flowering shrubs running parallel to the path that would put a smile on the most discouraged of visitors. At the bottom of the path, visitors were greeted by an array of colourful plants flowering at different times. Even if for a moment, this would help them forget the dreadful circumstances they were in.

A similar walk of shame mixed together with guilt led down to the inmate's entrance into the Visit Centre. I created another garden bed at the top of the hill that would be refreshing and cheerful when inmates arrived. The fellas loved it.

These beds, along with the roses and shrubs I'd planted in the rear gardens, all helped make the place more habitable. At the rear of the Visit Centre, I established some azalea beds on each side of the steps. Now when visitors and inmates alike stepped out onto the barbecue area and lawn, they were greeted by numerous healthy, vibrant plants that created a more cheerful environment.

On Saturdays and Sundays, before visitors arrived, I would pick a small bouquet of beautiful flowers and place them in a basic vase in the ladies' bathroom. Many commented on this, saying that it helped them forget the environment for a short while. It's funny what a few flowers can do to a person's outlook. They must have looked all right as I had them stolen on one visit day, container and all.

Why was this so important to me? Dhurringile is an out-of-the-way prison farm kilometres from nowhere on a lonely road, and visitors can't help feeling disheartened upon arrival. Many visitors required the prison bus to pick them up from the nearest railway station, which is why I made sure to keep it clean. Some wives and children stayed in the caravan park over the weekend. Others like Heather would drive up from Melbourne or some other town on one or both days to visit their men.

To put it in perspective, for a wife driving from Melbourne, that's five hours of travel by car both Saturday and Sunday as well as a long wait in line to get through the entrance, all for a three-hour visit. Heather did this every weekend without complaint. Not once did I hear her say, "You've got yourself into this mess," or "look what you're putting me through!"

My wife and all the other wives, children, parents, girlfriends, and other loved-ones who made such an effort on behalf of an inmate deserved anything that would add to their enjoyment of the visit.

22

Unusual Characters

Bender, the inmate who looked after the canteen in the Visit Centre, was also sympathetic to their cause. In his forties, Bender was serving a long sentence for murder. One late afternoon when Heather and the other visitors had all left, we poured ourselves a coffee and sat down for a short break before starting the clean-up. Through the huge glass windows, we could see the visitors departing up the flowered path to the right and the inmates walking up the left-hand pathway past their new gardens.

Our brief break turned into an hour as Bender began opening up about his history. He spoke fondly of his teen years in Tasmania and his family and much happier times. Then he touched on his profound regret over his crime of murder. "If he'd only said 'don't', I'd have spared his life."

He spoke matter-of-factly, but I could see deeper to the pain. My immediate thought was how a person's life could lie in the balance of a single word. Sadly, Bender didn't seem interested in letting God into his life. Our heavenly Father is the expert at wiping slates clean and removing pain, but Bender stopped at the edge, not even dipping his toe in the water of life. Prison visitors would never know just who was selling them sandwiches and drinks. That said, he was honest and had a real heart of compassion for the mums who were having it hard with their men inside.

I met a lot of unusual people during my time at Dhurringile. Darryl was one of the inmates who came to the Sunday evening New Wine Ministries church service. A long-term heroin user, Darryl generally did drug-related prison sentences of just a few months, then would be released, only to relapse and be back in prison within a short time. He was in twice during the few months I was at Dhurringile.

I wondered about Darryl's home, upbringing, and childhood. What had made him seek the comfort of heroin? Or did he just start trying it for recreation? I wondered why he used those two opposite forces to balance his life. The heroin in his veins when he was on the outside. Then prison to give him a forced break from heroin, allowing him to eat some regular food, go to gym, and build himself up again for the outside.

For some inmates, prison life is easier than facing the world outside prison walls. Inside, all their electricity, gas, food, water, and housing are taken care of by taxpayers. Coming up with money to cover those necessities on the outside is difficult. After all, who is going to give an ex-con druggie a job?

Many ex-inmates don't feel they fit in or are even wanted by society. In prison they have an identity, maybe even a position of respect and power among the other inmates. But who are they outside? Just an ex-con with a criminal record. Many withdraw, cutting themselves off from other people, rarely trying to change. Rejection is a painful emotion most people have felt at some time. But ex-inmates feel it even more, and they do not handle it well.

Non-prison people need greater understanding of some of the difficulties associated with incarceration. It isn't easy to automatically slot back into society after being removed from it for so long. Particularly if you didn't have a job in the first place when you were put inside, which accounts for more than sixty-five percent of male inmates. Who wants to hire a murderer, bank robber, rapist, or even a small-time thief? How does an ex-con hide their jail time on a résumé?

And if they do get a job, keeping it isn't easy either. In prison, inmates have to exhibit a certain toughness, a willingness to defend themselves. In the workplace, it's not about toughness but understanding people and working as a team, a complete reversal of the average inmate's persona. Darryl found that out numerous times. He'd try to go straight, but when that got too hard, he'd re-enter the drug scene to smother the pain of his conquered spirit. He'd just give up.

But this time when Darryl came inside and heard God's Word spoken, it struck a chord that was different from the past. This time he also had Christian support from me. Instead of carrying hate and anger with him throughout the prison, he carried a Bible and love everywhere. This new Darryl was a sight to behold, and he didn't care what people thought or said of him.

Darryl loved learning about God and never missed a Bible study or Sunday night NWM service. When he first came to my Bible studies, we were just commencing the Gospel of John. I read the opening passage.

> In the beginning was the Word, and the Word was with God, and the Word was God. He was in the beginning with God. All things were made through Him, and without Him nothing was made that was made. In Him was life, and the life was the light of men. And the light shines in the darkness, and the darkness did not comprehend it. (John 1:1-3)

Darryl had questions immediately. "What does that stuff mean about the Word?"

"Jesus is called the Word here," I explained. "We think of the world as being created by God. But here it says that Jesus, the Word, was in the beginning with God, and everything in and around the earth was made by the Word, Jesus. That includes all the stars and planets."

"How can that be if Jesus was born only 2000 years ago?" Darryl wanted to know.

"Well, that's because Jesus is God. Jesus was God from the beginning. God the Father, God the Son, or Jesus Christ, the Word, and God the Holy Spirit form the Holy Trinity, God in Three Persons. That's what these verses mean when they say Jesus, the Word, was both God and with God when the world was created. Have you heard of the Trinity?"

"Yes, of course," most of the group responded.

"As to life being in Jesus and that life being the light of men," I went on, "All human beings are sinful and therefore in darkness. Jesus is the light of the world because He alone can illuminate the way to heaven. Imagine a dark room with no light. That is our hearts and minds without Jesus. When we seek Jesus earnestly, and ask Him into our hearts, it's like someone switching on the light or lighting a candle. We are transformed from the inside out, enabling us to become children of God and live redeemed Christ-like lives."

As we studied, Darryl always had a contented smile that seemed to say God was changing him inside. But his sentence ended before we finished the study of John, and he was once again released.

Not long after my own release, I heard Darryl was back inside, this time at Beechworth Prison. I visited him, and he was as happy to see me as I was to see him. When we'd caught up a bit, I asked him with a half-smile, "Hey, what are you doing back inside?"

He looked sheepishly at the floor, then back at me. Through the toothless smile of a long-time opioid user, he replied as though sure I'd understand, "Aww, I dunno!"

And I did understand. After Darryl's release from Beechworth, I lost contact. I wanted to track him down on the outside to help keep his spiritual life alive, but though I searched the White Pages and rang many people with the same last name, I never found him. The last time I heard from Darryl was a couple of years after prison when he rang my home late one Saturday night. It gave Heather and me a fright as nobody rings at that time of night.

When I answered the phone, a man said, "Hi, it's Darryl!"

"Darryl who?" I asked, confused.

When he gave his full name, I realized who it was. Overjoyed, I asked, "How are you, mate?"

He mumbled some vague answers. I finally cut in. "Look, tell me where you are. We can get together and catch up."

He wouldn't reveal his whereabouts. Maybe I misread our conversation, but it felt as though he really needed to speak with me but was too embarrassed to meet face-to-face. He finally said goodbye and hung up. I continued searching for him off-and-on for the next several years to no avail.

But at least during his time in prison, he felt the power to overcome and did. Besides the Bible studies and NWM services, Darryl started meeting with us on Friday afternoons when Ted O'Brien from Prison Fellowship would visit.

Ted is another person I will never forget because of the impact he had on my life and so many other inmates. Regular as clockwork, rain, hail, or shine, Ted would be there every Friday to visit with the inmates. He was in his late forties and about my height of 5'7" with a perpetually friendly, caring smile and gentle, approachable personality. Prison visits took a lot of time out of his week, and we appreciated his company and wisdom. We loved Ted.

After I was released, I lost contact with him. Sometime later, I learned that he'd passed away. He was relatively young but had endured serious health problems that eventually caught up with him, much to my sorrow. There are people in life we just miss. To me, Ted was one of those. I'd love to have him back now just for a brew of coffee and a catch-up!

I'll never forget him telling me off once, gently, of course. What his rebuke added up to was that maybe I was a bit too fond of the sound of my own voice. I knew he loved me and wouldn't have brought up such a thing lightly. So instead of getting angry, I thanked him and became more aware of that fault from then on. I'm smiling even now as I write this thinking about the loving, kindly, discreet way he took me aside.

Thanks, Ted!

Around this time, a good friend from the past visited me. Michael was an ex-bank manager who felt called by God to start a Christian bookstore. Passionate for the Lord, he would sell Christian products in the front of the shop and have occasional guest speakers in the back.

During his visit, he mentioned that some churches were using my name and prison sentence to highlight what happens when a Christian backslides. He'd challenged one group when he heard them talking about me, asking, "Well, who among you has visited him in his predicament?"

He was referencing, of course, the biblical passages about visiting prisoners in their need (Hebrews 13:3; Matthew 25:34-45). The church folk involved were duly embarrassed. But I was embarrassed too, since I knew I was indeed an example of a backslidden Christian. I had to wonder if I'd have bothered visiting someone in prison myself if I were in the same position as those church people.

23

Change and Christmas

After Mick left 12 Dorm, a truly dark figure entered to take his place. This particular inmate had been incarcerated for some heavy stuff, and a sense of evil seemed to walk in behind him. I'd spoken to the guy many times before as he was already an inmate in a different dorm. But it wasn't until he moved into our room that I could really feel in my spirit the darkness and evil that emanated from him.

I prayed about it for a couple of days, wanting to give the guy a chance. But just as when I was in 8 Dorm, I felt a conviction in my spirit that it was time to leave as I didn't want to get side-tracked from what I was doing teaching Bible and sharing the gospel to engage in a hostile spiritual battle. I had enough battles as it was.

So I began praying for God to remove me from 12 Dorm. Within two days, God had answered even above what I could have hoped for. Packing my bags, I moved to an outside unit. You know you've made the big time when you're in the units!

Each large unit was big enough to fit two beds and wardrobes with enough room for a TV and kettle. The entire unit block was built in a U-shape that also housed the shower and toilet block. Unlike the mansion, these showers were individual cubicles instead of having to shower in a group. The single units were in the same block and about half the size of the double units.

The greater freedom and comfort of living in the units made me more appreciative of life's smaller blessings. Walking in the moonlight after dark, even if by myself instead of with my beautiful wife. Leaning on the unit balcony, looking up at the stars and breathing in the free air. Chatting to a mate outside over coffee instead of being locked into a dorm. All these were so different from my evenings in previous months of prison.

I started out sharing a double unit with the prison governor's own assigned gardener, Gerald, a great bloke and down-to-earth with a lovely wife and a couple of kids who thought the world of him. His prison sentence was for a one-time mistake for which he didn't even get paid before getting caught. And that is probably for the best.

Rooming with Gerald was a good experience. We had some brilliant discussions in the evenings, mainly about the reasons for life. He also began coming to Bible studies. I marked up a Gideon's Bible for him.

It was just a week before Christmas when I moved in with Gerald. That Christmas morning, a day neither of us had thought we'd be spending in prison, I asked him if he'd mind if I watched some Christmas preaching on TV. He had no objection, so I turned it to a Christmas service. We were both sitting up in our separate beds, reading Christmas cards from friends and family while listening to the TV when the preacher quoted a well-known Bible verse commonly referenced at Christmas.

> For unto us a child is born, unto us a son, is given, and the government shall be upon his shoulders, and his name shall be called Wonderful, Counsellor, the mighty God, the everlasting Father, the Prince of Peace. (Isaiah 9:6)

What the preacher actually said left out part of the verse, which was easy to pick up on if you know the passage well. Looking over at Gerald, I commented, "I think he left some words out of that verse!"

I proceeded to look the verse up in my Bible, then read the correct version back to him. Staring at me with a thunderstruck expression, he asked in an astounded tone, "You mean you know your Bible so well you actually know when a preacher leaves something out?"

I kept a straight face as if I was indeed the fountain of all knowledge. I didn't let on for days that it was actually a very common Bible passage to anyone who'd grown up celebrating Christmas in church. When I eventually confessed that I'd had that verse memorized since I was a kid so not exactly a sign of genius, we laughed and laughed.

Gerald then told me he should have educated himself biblically much earlier in life. In fact, it was Gerald who made a most interesting statement I wish I could hear from all humans. One evening we'd watched a story about Jesus on someone's TV, followed by a particular Bible study and discussion I delivered. When we finished, Gerald commented to me, "I've just realised that the Bible is life; past, present, and future!"

People don't come to that conclusion by themselves. That is only revealed by the Holy Spirit. Hearing that simple truth from a newcomer in the faith delighted me from the inside out and left me praising God.

Being in prison, there wasn't much I could do for a Christmas gift to my wife. But I saved up enough from my work to give her $50 when she arrived for a visit the Sunday after Christmas. It helped me feel I was contributing at least a little as a husband.

We dedicated our unborn child to God during that same visit right there in the Visit Centre with a hundred-plus other people celebrating their own family Christmas visits around us. I'd been dedicated in a similar way when I was an infant, and it was something Heather and I both thought important, following the biblical pattern of how the prophet Samuel's mother Hannah dedicated him to God (1 Samuel 1) and how Mary and Joseph presented baby Jesus to God in the temple (Luke 2:22-23).

Both Samuel and Jesus were special children born as the result of a miracle. Samuel to a barren woman. Jesus through the Holy Spirit to a virgin girl. Both were dedicated from birth to serve God. Samuel as Israel's prophet. Jesus, the Son of God, as the promised Messiah who would redeem and reconcile humanity to God through His death on the cross and resurrection.

To us, this child was also a very special gift from God even though we didn't know then that the daughter or son we were expecting would be our only child. We believed our child first and foremost belonged to God, and we wanted to rear this precious being in a manner befitting that. So right there quietly in the midst of the bustling Visit Centre, we prayed together, dedicating our child to God and to whatever God chose for the life and future of this daughter or son.

24

The Reaping

I'd been in the units about two months when I received news that my wife had been taken to the Shepparton Hospital birthing unit for the birth of our child.

The six weeks at the Parnells' house had come and gone quickly. Denys and Christine invited Heather to stay on in the house after they came back so she wouldn't have to move back to Melbourne. But Heather felt they needed the room for their own family, especially after such a long trip away. A few days before Denys and Christine were due to return, there was still nothing on the horizon regarding another place to live, so we both prayed about it.

Then Heather received a phone call from a new friend she'd made in Shepparton named Rena. A cousin of Heather's had introduced her to Rena while my wife was still driving up every weekend from Melbourne. Heather had gotten to know Rena well because Rena had insisted Heather stay over on Saturday nights instead of driving back exhausted to Melbourne, only to turn around and drive back in the morning.

Rena was looking for a housemate and suggested Heather

share a house with her for the remainder of her pregnancy and my prison sentence. With the Parnells on their way home, the timing couldn't be more perfect. And Rena was loving, patient, and understanding, the perfect friend with whom to finish off Heather's pregnancy and birth.

As to the house they moved into, it was originally built and lived in by a godly couple who had since passed away, making it extra-blessed for Heather. The couple had even added a little free-standing room out back to accommodate visiting preachers, similar to the Bible story of Elisha the prophet and the Shunamite woman who built him a "prophet's chamber" (2 Kings 4:8-37).

The prison officers kept me informed during the night as to Heather's condition. I'd be allowed two half-days of paternal leave to visit the hospital so long as I was a good inmate who followed the rules. I really wanted to be there for the birth, so the timing was everything. As they did their rounds, the updates from the prison officers were the same. "No news yet!"

My reply was also the same. "Thanks, boss."

Many of the officers were fathers themselves, so they were kind and helpful to a new father, even an inmate. Heather came from a family of five, and my family had six siblings. So we'd both expected to have a small football team of children ourselves with this one being the first. We were, of course, both wrong.

When it was time for the birth, the prison officers raced me to the hospital. I ended up missing the delivery by a half-hour. But I was there in time to be the first to wash my new son. What a fantastic experience washing this little bundle of orange joy in a tub not much bigger than he was.

Yes, I said orange! Though all had gone well with the natural birth my wife wanted, our child had an orange tinge that didn't seem natural. We found out that he was jaundiced, which would require a full blood transfusion if other treatments didn't work. This meant he'd have to remain in the hospital for eight days instead of the usual two days. He looked so helpless, and there was nothing we could do but pray. We immediately rang both our families for prayer.

I was instinctively concerned about my son, and having only two half-days of leave meant it would be back to mere phone calls to communicate with Heather. It made me feel like jumping into one of the prison's cars and driving to the hospital myself as I'd done with Dad's car when I visited him.

Then to my astonishment, another miracle happened. I'd always thought the prison governor didn't like me, despite the positive outcome of the Minister of Corrections' visit. So I was flabbergasted when he told the prison officers, "Any time you've got someone going into Shepparton, put Neyland on board. Anyone like him who does the right thing by the prison, I'll do the right thing by him!"

I nearly fell over in shock when the officers told me about it. During the eight days my son and wife were in the hospital, I was released for five total visits. Afternoon after afternoon, officers would put me on board a car, bus, or truck, drop me off at the hospital for a few hours, then do their errands and pick me up on the way back. On day one, the officers took us all to the Swim/Gym pool around noon. As we got out of the bus, the officer said, "Neyland, you stay on board."

He dropped me off at the hospital and picked me up at around 3:30 p.m. Fantastic! The next day, another officer was going into Shepparton for prison groceries.

"Hey Neyland, you come with me," he ordered. "I'll need a hand with all this stuff."

Instead, he dropped me off at the hospital. The following day was my rostered paternal day, with Denys and Christine Parnell taxiing me, and I went in two further afternoons in the coming days.

Meanwhile, my new-born son was doing his own hard sentence in his own prison of a humidicrib. We'd named him Niven Lewis Neyland. Lewis was my brother John's middle name. He hadn't responded to natural sun treatment to correct his blood deficiencies. After several days of coughing, jaundice, and getting weaker, he was finally given a full transfusion.

We haven't got a clue whose blood it was. But we are grateful as he wouldn't be here with us if not for that. So give blood! Donating blood saves lives!

I am so thankful for those visits as this whole ordeal was really getting to Heather. She'd been on the front line since I'd gone to court, finishing off all the things left undone when I went inside and dealing with various issues from the business. On top of that, she'd experienced several robberies, gone through pregnancy without a husband of any use, and moved by herself to a new town hundreds of kilometres away while living on a pension.

Adding on a dangerously ill new-born son piled on pressure to the exploding point. A couple of times, out of hours, she ended up calling the prison office in tears, sobbing into the phone, "May I please speak to Niven?"

The prison officers were always good to us, "I'll get a message to him, Mrs Neyland, and we'll let him ring you back from the office."

Thankfully, Heather's mum Lyn came down to Shepparton to help her. She was Heather's rock and great comfort as was Rena, a very special girl sent by God at a particular time.

While I was away from the prison, Gerald pitched in with my chores. He was a great help, assisting me with various things like watering the plants and cleaning up the Visit Centre. My Christian inmate friend Trevor also took the pressure off me, helping where he could. Having been in various prisons over the years, Trevor told me, "Niven, this amount of paternal leave is unheard of in the prison system."

I made sure to thank the prison governor. He just smiled and responded with, "I don't know a thing about it!" But I knew what he'd done, and he knew I was grateful. I guess he really had appreciated all the work I'd done in improving the grounds.

Over the following days, I felt quite helpless about being a dad. Here I was in prison feeling absolutely pathetic as a husband, and my family might as well have been a continent away for all the use I was to them. Another inmate told me, "you've been showing signs of strain for about a week now." I hit rock bottom a few times within myself in that time period. But I had to keep my head about me and make it sound to Heather as if everything was all right. Husbands are meant to be a comfort and pillar of strength to their wives, and I had to be that for Heather.

God again showed us great love and mercy. Fred and Audrey, a friendly older Christian couple who lived next door to Rena and Heather, were like godly, sweet grandparents. They would pop over for cups of tea and invite the girls over to their home for a meal. Between Rena, Fred, and Audrey, as well as my mother-in-law until she returned home, Heather had great built-in babysitters, which allowed her plenty of much-needed rest. Fred and Audrey used to walk Niv Jr. up and down the street just so Heather could lie down, put her feet up, and close her eyes.

I was really needing a change in my living situation as well. Though Gerald had been a terrific roommate, living in a double unit had its problems for me. I liked rising early so I could start studying, praying, and preparing for the day. That was difficult to do without waking Gerald. I'd been praying about it, and God once again answered my prayers almost immediately.

Another inmate and friend Dyson had a single unit but preferred to be in a double unit with some company. He and Gerald got on well, and he knew I ran Bible studies and needed my own space. So he offered me a swap. For the first time since A Division six months earlier, I was by myself. I could pray, read, or listen to Christian music any time I wanted without TV or other interruptions.

I acquired a small desk, and Heather brought me a lamp. From there, I began getting up at 5:00 a.m. to pray and do Bible study before the busy days commenced. I could also counsel inmates going through difficult times in privacy. It was a wonderful change, and I stayed in that single unit until the end of my sentence.

Niven Jr. was born almost exactly four months before I was released and was indeed the greatest gift any couple could receive. God's goodness defies all logic and understanding, and His mercy has no end. His heart is large beyond measure, and He enjoys blessing where he can.

25

Plom's Disease

Inmate families find life hard when the partner or father is inside. It's challenging for a wife and mother to become both father and mother, financial controller, provider of all things spiritual, emotional, and physical. Especially to kids who are often too young to understand or too resentful to help. All week, these mothers work hard to maintain some resemblance of normal life. Then on weekends when they should be resting, they have to travel the long journey to meet their inmate hubby at the prison, who has quite likely just come in from a game of tennis, coffee break, or shower.

One inmate who attended New Wine Ministries Sunday services requested prayer for his wife. She was in the last stage of pregnancy and having serious health problems. She was already rundown in both body and mind due to having recently broken her arm and caring for her two other children. Now she was under threat of her electricity and phone being cut off because she had no money to pay the bills.

Those were real problems and quite typical of situations in which many prison families found themselves. Seeing families like this quickly healed me of PLOM's Disease. i.e., Poor Little Old Me!

Poor Little Old Me is a disease reflecting a lack of maturity. It gets into most inmates or ex-inmates at some stage as well as many people who've never entered the prison system. You know someone has PLOM's Disease when you find them constantly whining and whinging about something in their lives. Different day, different story but always the same theme—Poor Little Old Me!

I'd read about PLOM's disease in a book and first noticed I had a touch of it while walking past the inmate-use phones at the rear of the prison offices. Another inmate was on the phone, yelling and swearing at his wife. I'd seen his wife and kids on visits, and she sure didn't deserve that kind of talk and lack of respect. I told myself I should have a word with the guy.

Then a strong sense of understanding came over me that was obviously from God. I began thinking of all the whining I'd done since being in prison, belly-aching about this and that. I'd thought I'd been Christian enough to pray for my spiteful ex-sister-in-law, choosing to leave everything in God's hands. Now I felt embarrassed and selfish at my judgemental criticism of this guy.

In truth, nothing I was going through compared to the predicament he and his wife were in. He'd been locked up for months, leaving his wife to get their three kids fed and dressed for school every day, earn a living, nurse them when they were sick, and get them on a train every weekend to visit dad. Not to mention dealing with all the household bills. Meanwhile, I had a lovely wife, a new-born baby, and just a few loose ends to deal with. That realisation led me to permanently give up PLOM's Disease.

It also gave me a new perspective on Jesus's words about His coming as the Good Shepherd.

> The thief does not come except to steal, and to kill, and to destroy. I have come that they may have life, and that they may have it more abundantly. I am the good shepherd. The good shepherd gives His life for the sheep. (John 10:10-11)

I noticed that this scripture is two-sided. The thief, Satan rules the negative side that steals your joy, kills your love, and destroys your life. Jesus Christ, the Good Shepherd, rules the other side, which allows us to throw off all the negative baggage like our personal hurts and bitterness and live for Christ in the abundance of a newly generated life. From the moment I flipped that mental coin over with the abundant side facing up, I began really living for Christ. In doing so, I found that abundant life Christ promises right in the heart of the prison.

Praise God for His freedom! I now understood what the apostle Paul said when he intimated that a Christian can't really be a prisoner because wherever we are with Christ, we are free (2 Timothy 2:9). Our mind is free, our heart is free, and to some extent our mouth is free. So God doesn't want to hear our whining over what we've missed out on or what we feel robbed of, especially after we've been set free from the prison of those memories.

I am called to show Christ in both my actions and with my words. How can I do that if I'm whinging about stuff? I've been brought out of darkness into His marvellous light, and yet sometimes I was still talking as if I were back in that darkness!

The more I thought about it, the more I realised my PLOM Disease could be a real stench to listeners because it didn't exhibit the consistent faith and trust I wanted to demonstrate as a mature Christian. I thought of the biblical patriarch Job, who was famed for his patience under trial (James 5:11). He'd not only lost all his children and wealth but was covered in terrible sores and boils, and yet he could say with complete faith and without blaming God:

> Naked I came from my mother's womb, and naked shall I return there. The Lord gave, and the Lord has taken away; Blessed be the name of the Lord. (Job 1:21)

Just what is the attraction of PLOM's Disease? For one, there is a certain pleasure in whining. I find that if I begin, I don't seem to stop. Everybody wants others to feel sorry for them, and we all have a story to tell of some wrong being done to us. The trouble is that we rarely tell stories of how we have wronged others. We tend to leave the ugly sides of ourselves out of our tale of woe. Yet we all have those as well.

We've all done someone wrong at some time. We have all done or thought things only God knows about and that we hope He doesn't tell anyone. We find it easy to leave those bits out of our life story, that part of the truth about ourselves.

When our journey is full of whining rather than the glory of God, we are still spiritual children, drinking milk instead of solid spiritual food, for which the apostle Paul once scolded the Corinthian church.

> Brothers and sisters, I could not address you as people who live by the Spirit but as people who are still worldly—mere infants in Christ. I gave you milk, not solid food, for you were not yet ready for it. Indeed, you are still not ready. You are still worldly. For since there is jealousy and quarrelling among you, are you not worldly? Are you not acting like mere humans? (1 Corinthians 3:1-3; see also 1 Peter 2:1-2).

For some of us, every issue and shortage of anything in our lives is always someone else's fault. It's an immature way of living life. We can't partake of solid Scripture like adults do because that means growing up and stopping the complaining. In healing me of PLOM's Disease, God was calling me to be more robust in spirit. To be able to handle all sorts of issues and problems coming from an array of angles. Part of growing up as a Christian is being built up spiritually to weather all categories of life's storms. All of them! It's like the apostle Paul said from a prison cell:

> I know what it is to be in need, and I know what it is to have plenty. I have learned the secret of being content in any and every situation, whether well fed or hungry, whether living in

plenty or in want. I can do all this through him [Christ] who gives me strength. (Philippians 4:12-13)

If I am a mature Christian, I should be able to handle being rich or poor. I should be able to maintain my dignity whether in prison or out of prison. I should be able to keep my humility whether in places of high esteem or being a nobody. I won't be blaming someone else every time something changes in my life.

Instead, I can ride it through, knowing that Christ Jesus was able to do it and that His expectation for me is to do the same. He endured! I endure!

You see, I am not a mature man until I take responsibility for my failures and the consequences arising from them. As was clear after my collision, some decisions I'd made had serious consequences, and I was called to be accountable for them. My collision was forced accountability. What God wants is for us to offer that accountability voluntarily.

Many people always find excuses for failing their spouses, families, and friends. Until we throw those excuses in the trash bin, stand up like real men and women, and be accountable for every action we apply to life, we are still trying to live like a child who says, "I'm not responsible for this." Once I acknowledged that the buck stopped with me, I began to admit that I had no excuse. I'd simply failed in some of my choices. Once I was willing to admit whose choice it was—mine—and face the music, that's when I began to grow up spiritually.

Just think of who God put in charge of the nation of Israel

when He freed them from captivity in Egypt. Moses was a man of real maturity with forty years of experience as a prince of Egypt and forty years as a shepherd of sheep. But he went through a lot of trials and immaturity before God considered him capable of being used to lead the Israelites, including being rejected by his own people and banished from Egypt as a murderer (Exodus 2).

I wonder how many times during those forty years in the wilderness he thought of himself as a failure. We certainly see such thoughts when he told God he was too slow of speech and tongue to be a leader to the Israelites (Exodus 4:10). The Bible doesn't tell us in detail how Moses had to fight all those decades through his spiritual infancy and youth to become a man in his mind and heart before he was ready to be called for God's purpose. But God made certain of Moses's maturity even when Moses wasn't sure of himself or his own abilities.

In the same way, I needed to defeat PLOM Disease by throwing all reasons for whining in the trash bin and leave them there. Satan wants to put his thoughts into our hearts, so we can whine and bleat about all the wrongs in life we think we are suffering. That is why we are commanded:

> Keep your heart with all diligence, for out of it are the issues of life. (Proverbs 4:23)

In other words, it was my responsibility to protect and keep my heart for the peace of God to reside in it, not to indulge in immature lamb-bleats of where I felt I'd been short-changed. There's a very well-known poem written by the famous

British author and poet Rudyard Kipling I find worthy of recalling when I'm tempted to whinge and whine. Like me, this poem may mean a lot to you. To me, it's about growing from a child into a mature person.

IF

By Rudyard Kipling

If you can keep your head when all about you
Are losing theirs and blaming it on you,
If you can trust yourself when all men doubt you,
But make allowance for their doubting too;
If you can wait and not be tired by waiting,
Or being lied about, don't deal in lies,
Or being hated, don't give way to hating,
And yet don't look too good, nor talk too wise:

If you can dream—and not make dreams your master;
If you can think—and not make thoughts your aim;
If you can meet with Triumph and Disaster
And treat those two impostors just the same;
If you can bear to hear the truth you've spoken
Twisted by knaves to make a trap for fools,
Or watch the things you gave your life to, broken,
And stoop and build them up with worn-out tools:

If you can make one heap of all your winnings
And risk it on one turn of pitch-and-toss,
And lose, and start again at your beginnings
And never breathe a word about your loss;

If you can force your heart and nerve and sinew
To serve your turn long after they are gone,
And so hold on when there is nothing in you
Except the Will which says to them: 'Hold on!'

If you can talk with crowds and keep your virtue,
Or walk with Kings—nor lose the common touch,
If neither foes nor loving friends can hurt you,
If all men count with you, but none too much;
If you can fill the unforgiving minute
With sixty seconds' worth of distance run,
Yours is the Earth and everything that's in it,
And—which is more—you'll be a Man, my son!

26

More Unique People

One day a long-term inmate packing up to be released discovered he had an entire black garbage bag full of Gideon's Bibles stashed in a locker. Bringing them to me, he asked, "Hey, Niv, can you use any of these?"

"Absolutely, mate!" I replied. "I could have used these months ago!"

I began distributing the thirty-odd Bibles around the prison, putting them in the dorms and units. No one objected except one guy who, like the bannister kicker, felt he needed to act like a tough guy. Entering the dorm, I gave my usual spiel. "G'day, fellas! I'll just put these Bibles on the bookshelves for anyone who wants to read them."

As I turned to leave, the guy got up from his bed, walked over to the Bibles, and grabbed one. Following me out of the room, he threw it, hitting me right in at the back of my head, all the while yelling unprintable language. It's amazing how many thoughts can go through one's head in a split second. I wanted to throw off my cloak of Christian righteousness, leap at him, and give him a beating, which would probably have made him a much more malleable person very quickly. Better all-around, in fact.

I just about had to nail my feet to the floor to stop myself. In the space of a few milliseconds, I'd gone from zero to ten on the rage scale—from peaceful, friendly Christian leader to thug. Thankfully, I got rid of the rage as quickly as it came and kept calm, not saying a thing. I just picked up the thrown Bible and put it in someone else's dorm.

The guy actually turned out not to be so bad. He even came to Sunday night church a few times. I invited him to Bible studies and spoke to him about salvation, but he didn't want to take it any further. He was just scared, uncomfortable in his own skin, and had watched way too many prison movies, so he felt he needed to act like a tough guy. During my sentence, I never saw anyone look more like a fish out of water in prison than that guy.

Some prisoners really were tough guys. Sometime after my son's birth, I'd started a news bulletin I'd dubbed the *Dhurringile Christian Blurb*. Not the fanciest of names, but it announced all the various Christian activities in the prison such as services, Bible studies, and prayer meetings. My Christian friend Trevor had a computer, so he helped with layout and printing. I would give a copy to new prisoners arriving on the "Dhurringile Express."

One particular newcomer was a redhead about forty, at least six-foot, two, and extremely fit. He had numerous tattoos on his body, including his knuckles and backs of his hands. But for me, the distinguishing tattoos were the two spider webs on his elbows.

Handing him a copy of the bulletin, I said in a friendly tone, "Here ya go, mate. This will tell you about all the Christian stuff going on in the prison."

He quickly eyed me up and down, took the bulletin with an expressionless thanks, and kept walking. Despite the warrior appearance, the guy was quiet and kept to himself. Then one day after a muster as the guards were walking away, he attacked another guy without any warning at all. It was like someone had let a hurricane out of a cupboard.

Within seconds, he'd beaten the other guy to a pulp. Then he spun around to see if anyone else wanted a taste. Nobody did. In the end, it was the beaten guy who got shanghaied back to a walled prison. He was a major troublemaker who'd caused a lot of problems around the prison. Niggling that redhead turned out to be his big mistake!

Another inmate, Stretch, was a bit like me in that he was raised in a Christian family who had godly aims for him but got caught up in a non-church crowd, recreational drugs, then struggled with harder stuff. Now that his temptations were outside the prison, Stretch was able to concentrate on his deeper desire of following God. He was the only inmate I could talk to who had been brought up in church from a child as I was. We'd learned the same songs, heard similar sermons, and Stretch was familiar with topics I drew from in Bible studies.

Another inmate who became a good friend was Neville.

Muscular with a large tattoo of an eagle on his back and a few other scattered tattoos dating from his teens, he had scald marks on his face that made him look more fearsome than he was. Sentenced to prison the first time at just twenty years old, and worried about someone forcing him to be their new prison boyfriend, he was reassured by one old timer, "Don't worry, son! Your face will protect your body!"

Many years later, Neville found himself inside again. As he got off the bus, I handed him and his co-arrivals a copy of the *Dhurringile Christian Blurb*. Interestingly, of all the bulletins I gave out to arriving prisoners, not one of them threw it back at me and only one turned it down with a polite, "No thanks!"

In truth, I've found prison to be a place where God does some of His best work. He can reach down into any dark pit to touch the human soul, and He was reaching people here. I would certainly never have come to prison voluntarily. I had to be dragged here by legislation and a judge's gavel. But God worked greatly in my life through my incarceration just as I witnessed in so many other lives.

Prison is the devil's playground. But ironically, it is also where the prisoner is removed far enough from his daily temptations to concentrate on the deeper issues of life. Given the right words and tools, many inmates will do just that. Others just go through the motions of incarceration, biding their time without so much as a thought of living a better existence. While many don't even try, others simply don't understand how.

When Neville arrived, he was an angry beast. In fact, he was the angriest person I'd laid eyes on anywhere. In his early days at Dhurringile, his face was red with anger most of the time. One day by chance, I started walking with Neville around the 700-metre track. I was just a few metres ahead, quietly praising God. Suddenly, I heard a voice cursing and mumbling swear words behind me.

When I turned around, I saw that it was Neville, so I slowed my pace just enough for him to catch up. As he was about to pass me, I said, "Hi. Do you want someone to walk with?"

Without waiting for his response, I began to keep pace with him. For the next several laps, all I heard was cursing and telling me about the people he wanted to punch, slap, or beat up. Lap after lap, the anger poured out of him like an endless lava torrent of hatred discharging from his heart. I hadn't realized anyone could build up such a reservoir of wrath.

After that, I walked with Neville regularly. He spent lap after lap cursing about those who'd done him wrong. His wife, friends, workmates, or other inmates—nobody escaped his vitriolic mumblings. Proverbs 15:1 tells us that "a soft answer turns away wrath," so I kept speaking softly to him, asking gentle questions, talking about forgiveness and better times ahead. In time, I introduced the topic of Jesus and what He can do.

Slowly but surely over the coming days, the anger drained out of Neville to the point that he began smiling and laughing at jokes and kidding around. Whatever had bound him to all that animosity, it was clear he'd been freed and we had a new Neville. I invited him to Sunday night church, which he attended and enjoyed. I also invited him to Ted's Prison Fellowship meeting and my own Bible studies. In fact, he came to everything that was about God.

Then I got him a Gideon's Bible, underlining specific scriptures as I'd done for others. That was where we ran into trouble, as it turned out Neville was dyslexic and had difficulty reading. I told him many people had overcome reading disabilities and changed their lives. He booked into the prison education classes, a bit embarrassed to be starting at a Grade 3 level, but he worked hard and learned how to read properly.

God had miraculously changed Neville's nature. Upon arrival, he was such an angry man. A few months later, he was a peaceful bloke seeking Jesus Christ, his anger replaced by love and fun. This newly-changed Neville would now help wherever he could and smiled wherever he went.

Neville eventually began carrying his Bible around the prison, reading it every time he wasn't working. He had this glow on his face that communicated without words what God was doing to his heart. If I hadn't seen it in person, I wouldn't have believed it. It reminded me of how the Bible describes the radiance of Moses's face when he came down from Mount Sinai after meeting with God and receiving the Ten Commandments (Exodus 34:29-35).

On one of her visits, Neville's wife came over to me in

the Visit Centre Hall, tears of joy in her eyes. Giving me a hug, she asked, "Niven, what have you done with Neville? He writes me a love letter every night! I don't understand the change, but I can't thank you enough. I have my husband back, and I'm in love with him again."

"It's not me," I told her. "The change is due to the Holy Spirit moving in his life."

Neville became liked and appreciated by most people in the prison and a good mate to me personally. After I was released, I was able to help get Neville a job. We even had Bible studies for a while with his family.

27

Anger Management

During a conversation with my close Christian mate Trevor, I raised the topic of anger. I'd noticed how many prisoners were incarcerated for anger-related crimes. Trevor was well-aware since his own crime was anger-related. So many inmates would not be in here if they'd just controlled their anger at a particular moment.

Trevor and I began working on an anger-management course we could offer Dhurringile inmates. Trevor's computer skills helped enormously, and he had a lot of relevant input from his own personal past and experiences from various prisons he'd been in. We both believed that anger was a learned behaviour that could be unlearned, given the right opportunity and tools.

One helpful research book I found was Steve Biddulph's *The Secret of Happy Children*, which highlights the damage the tongue can do and the fatal power of negative talk. It also emphasises the importance of positive, uplifting speech and the choices we make in how we present words to people.

"You're so stupid! . . . You're such a selfish person! . . . You fool, stop it! . . . You moron! You are such a pest to be around!" These are all negative terms often spoken recklessly with only one result— negative performance from the receiver of such language. The apostle James describes the problem of negative talk vividly.

> Consider what a great forest is set on fire by a small spark. The tongue also is a fire, a world of evil among the parts of the body. It corrupts the whole body, sets the whole course of one's life on fire, and is itself set on fire by hell. All kinds of animals, birds, reptiles and sea creatures are being tamed and have been tamed by mankind, but no human being can tame the tongue. It is a restless evil, full of deadly poison. With the tongue we praise our Lord and Father, and with it we curse human beings, who have been made in God's likeness. Out of the same mouth come praise and cursing. My brothers and sisters, this should not be. (James 3:5b-10)

Some people have an inexplicable expectation that negative talk produces a positive effect. Woefully, many of those are parents. They ruin their children's view of themselves from an early age with that kind of talk, then wonder why their kids don't perform like the winners they hoped they would be.

The bottom line is that information fed into the subconscious will habitually come out in our actions. Jesus gave us a hint of the impact a parent has on children in speaking of His own relationship with the Father.

> The Son can do nothing of Himself, but what He sees the Father do; for whatever He does, the Son also does in like manner. (John 5:19)

Negative or positive, a child will mostly mimic the words and actions of the parents. If there is negative talk and abuse around the home, children will pick that up like magnets pick up iron filings. When they in turn have children, they will most likely do and say the same to their own kids. Parents are fooling themselves if they think children will pick up anything other than what they see and hear.

I had a workplace manager many years ago who shouldn't have been a manager. I don't know how his own children ended up, but his workers put up with all sorts of cheap insults. Every time a worker or team brought a completed job for sign-off, some smart remark sprinkled with mocking and ridicule would be already spilling from his lips. He may have just started out using a bit of workplace sarcasm, and it just grew from there like a wildfire he couldn't put out once it started. Being the boss, I guess he saw no reason to put it out.

Many inmates had grown up under people like him, parents like him, relatives like him, and the insults and disparaging comments had taken their evil toll. All their lives, they'd been told, "You'll never amount to anything." Now they were living out that testimony prophesied over them.

As authors Ken Blanchard and Spencer Johnson point out in their title *One Minute Manager*: "People do good work when they feel good about themselves." This became the premise of our anger-management course *Anger, Is It You?* We ran it late afternoon Monday through Friday with homework in the evenings.

The prison's second-in-command opened the course

personally with a formal speech to all attending. He was thrilled that inmates had researched, developed, and were prepared to run this course for other inmates. Then each participant shared what they were willing to share of their life story. Some clearly felt ashamed and saddened hearing their own words. Their painful stories broke my own heart.

We discussed how justifiable anger compares with unjustifiable anger. We also bored down into the anger that arises in specific incidents and situations. At the end of the first session, Trevor and I told the attendees that this was an anger-management course, not a spelling or grammar class. So if anybody had problems filling in answers on their homework sheets, they could come to my unit or Trevor's for assistance.

That evening, I was stunned to find five attendees lined up in front of my unit while Trevor had three in front of his. Illiteracy is sadly common among inmates, and we were seeing it first-hand in our course. We had to rethink the pace with which we covered the course material to ensure they all kept up.

One such attendee was twenty-two-year-old Jimmy, who was incarcerated for constant, violent fighting. He was a good-looking, friendly sort of kid, who at first glance seemed to have no real problem except the need to grow up and learn some self-control. Then he shared part of his story.

His parents had fought a lot until their marriage fell apart while Jimmy was still in primary school. They argued about which one loved their children best, who did the most work, and who brought in the most money. This left Jimmy feeling angry and rejected. By the end of primary school, he was already getting into fights. After their separation, his behaviour worsened.

When he entered secondary school, the reason for his fighting was misdiagnosed. What the school thought was typical disruptive behaviour was actually trauma-related dysphoria. In other words, his learning abilities had shut down due to the family issues he'd experienced as a child. To make matters worse, the teachers got rid of the problem he'd become by just passing him at the end of each school year.

"A pass is a good thing, isn't it?" I queried.

"Not when you don't know anything!" he replied. "Every year, I brought my worries from home to school, which made it hard to concentrate on the lessons. I tried hard to get my brain to work, but it just wouldn't! It was like my brain was covered with plastic and everything the teacher said just washed off. I felt dumb so I started playing up and got into fights."

"So were there any subjects you actually enjoyed learning?" I asked.

"Yeah, most of them," Jimmy responded. "I really wanted to learn. I just wish they could have slowed down. But I just kept getting passed to the next grade, and the further behind I got, the more hopeless and useless I felt. When I left school after Year 11, my certificate said I was educated and ready for the workforce. But in truth, I couldn't write a decent sentence or do basic maths."

Doing some research, I discovered that Jimmy's situation was a typical response to young age trauma. The brain enters a perpetual survival mode, locking out all learning of new things. What that meant for Jimmy was that his trauma interfered with his psychological and social skills. It also affected problem-solving, memorisation, attention span, effective communication, as well as controlling his temper. These were all behaviours necessary for success in the classroom as well as in adult life. Under less unhappy circumstances, Jimmy might have been as competent as any other student.

We based much of our anger-management course on the Bible, which speaks a lot about anger and its effect. No one complained about our use of Scripture. I think they were just pleased to get some help from people who understood where they were at.

One interesting statistic that came to light during the course was that a good forty percent of attendees had fathers who drank alcohol and were angry and violent. This behaviour was passed down to their sons, who were now dealing with the same issues of anger and violence in their own lives and families. Two-thirds of the men in our group were already divorced.

Many anger-related murders are simply because someone went a step too far in an argument, misunderstanding, or even a thought. There is a very narrow gap between a close call and a prison sentence. And the only difference between an inmate and someone who hasn't been to prison is often just that the latter hasn't yet been caught in their violent outbursts of anger.

Over the five days, we worked our way methodically through the material. The attendees were so enthusiastic they asked for a sixth day, which the prison governor granted. At the end of the course, thanks to Trevor's computer skills, we gave each participant an attractive certificate of participation with their name on it.

28

Free At Last!

The final three months of my ten-month incarceration were the busiest. I was running the anger management course with Trevor, teaching a couple of Bibles studies a week, running a prayer meeting, holding down a job, as well as taking a couple of educational courses. I was also counselling other inmates and doing personal Bible studies with some of them.

A visit from Prison Fellowship representative Ted O'Brien added to my workload. He introduced Trevor and me to well-known Shepparton Christian basketball player Dallas Terlich, who was representing a local church that wanted to start a basketball competition for prison inmates. The proposition was for two mixed teams of inmates and local Christian basketball players to play each other Friday nights in Shepparton for a six-week season, followed by a trophy night back at the prison that would include a music band and food. If all went well, there would be a second season.

Once the prison agreed to the competition, I became the inside man to do advertising and get inmate teams ready to go. We had no problem finding players, since this meant getting out of prison for a night. In fact, Trevor and I were both surprised to find we had so many good players at Dhurringile. Some had even played at a respectable competition level for good clubs on the outside. While I'm far from a good player, I made the team though mainly, I'm guessing, because I was the round-up boss.

The trophy night was a winner with a terrific music band and a short but loving and powerful message of hope in Christ. Spurred on by the free food, the place was packed with players and non-players alike. Sport is a great release of testosterone for men, and the prison governor remarked that it had been a great success. Between Dallas, Trevor, and me, we set down a good pattern for future competitions, and they lasted long after I was released.

That said, my job of getting players ready wasn't easy. Part of the competition agreement was that each team player had to be at the office ready for the bus trip. I was amazed that some would still be on their beds watching TV or having a smoke when it was time to go. Or they'd decide at the last minute they couldn't be bothered, having no consideration of responsibility or commitment to the team.

Their indifference annoyed me, but I also knew this type of decision-making was why many were inside in the first place, so I had to approach the solution wisely. Instead of telling them off, I'd encourage them as to how important and valuable they were to the team. While some days were difficult, I always got them across the finish line even if it meant holding up the bus for a few minutes.

Nearing the end of my sentence, I had an unusual experience. The prison had selected a few trusted inmates to go to the movies, lollies, ice creams, and all. Though we were in civilian clothing, I felt like I had a neon sign above my head shouting "PRISONER!"

In truth, we just looked like a group of guys attending a movie together, and no one paid us any attention. It was just a reaction to being out of the public eye for so long. Crazily, six out of the nine of us were murderers. Neville, who was part of the group, commented that if we wanted a bit more elbow room, we could announce that over the loudspeaker. Not really funny but probably true.

About this time, Trevor gave me some sound advice I've passed on to many others since. "Niv, this is just a caution. When people get close to the end of their sentences, they start opening their mouths and spurting out all the things they've wanted to say but didn't dare. Problem is, they end up getting their mouths closed by someone else."

He may have seen something in me I hadn't or was just making a suggestion. I didn't ask, but I heeded his word of warning and made sure to keep my mouth controlled as I got closer to my release date. Overall, I'd built several solid relationships inside, and though I was overjoyed to be leaving, I would have liked to shove some of those guys in a bus and take them with me.

Just before getting out, I handed my basketball role over to the son of one of Melbourne's most notorious gangsters. Despite his background and his own criminal history, he was competent, fit, personable, and educated, and I was blessed to have him.

I also handed over my great Visit Centre job, recommending to the governor a mate who'd assured me he'd look after all the gardens and landscaping I'd put in. Sadly, when I visited Dhurringile just a couple of months after my release, the first thing I noticed walking down the visitors path was the absence of all the plants I'd worked so hard to grow there. The mate had cut them down to grass level as he'd decided it was too hard to water them. All for the sake of not spending a half hour twice a week. Time he would have clearly had.

I was both angry and disappointed. Those plants were for the families and played a therapeutic role for visitors. During my visit, I spoke to the guy about my disappointment, but he just laughed it off. The lesson for me was that I couldn't let my feelings get dragged down by all the effort so many people had invested to get these plants in and growing. Dhurringile Prison Farm was no longer my home, and this was just one more thing I needed to just leave behind and walk away from.

Besides spending Christmas and my thirty-seventh birthday inside, the second anniversary of John's death came just a couple of weeks before my release. The following is my diary entry from that day.

> Two years since John died. I had many things planned for today but had to ditch them all except prayer and memories. I miss John immensely, and not a day goes by that when I think on

him my eyes water just short of crying. I realise that I am still devastated by his death and am hoping that recent findings have a bearing on the future. If I were single now, I'd be a wreck.

As a strange comfort, I noticed on a desk calendar I used in prison the following inscription for that day. Even now, it's still stuck fast in the front of my Bible, and I read it during times of reflection for comfort.

> And even to your old age, I am He, and even to your grey hairs will I carry you! I have made and I will bear; even I will carry you and will deliver you. (Isaiah 46:4)

So far, God has kept that promise, and I have absolute confidence He always will!

The morning of my release, Heather arrived at Dhurringile Prison Farm on the dot of 6:00 a.m. I was waiting in the front office, shaved and showered, my bags ready, and my release papers signed. The prison officers expressed both happiness and sadness that I was leaving and sent me off with several compliments for my contributions during my time there. But they also added, "We don't want to see you back here!"

I smiled in agreement. I planned to be back but not as a prisoner. After a few goodbyes, I put my bags in the boot of Heather's little blue Datsun, and off Heather and I went. As we drove past the farm, I had the feeling of sorrow and loss we experience when leaving something precious behind. Despite being in prison, I'd had a lot of special days with special people.

But my mind quickly snapped back to my new freedom

as Heather raced through the gears and floored the gas as though in the Monaco Grand Prix. I think she'd had enough of prison for one lifetime. There we were, my wife, my infant son, and me, a few bags, and a tank full of gas heading off into the dawn of a new era.

Two and a half hours later, we arrived in Sydenham. My sister Beth had put on a big breakfast and invited lots of friends and family to celebrate my release. She'd also put a yellow ribbon around a tree in the front yard like the Tony Orlando classic song, *Tie a Yellow Ribbon Round the Ole Oak Tree*, about a prisoner returning home from prison and not sure he will be welcome. She'd thought it would be a nice homecoming touch. But as we turned onto Beth's street and I saw all the people in the front yard waving madly and waiting to welcome me back to society, I just couldn't face them yet.

"Keep driving!" I barked at Heather. "I'm not going in."

I'd faced these same people in prison as visitors, so I didn't understand my sudden overwhelming fear. It wasn't the embarrassment I'd thought I might feel, but something else associated with incarceration I couldn't quite put my finger on. I am fortunate that Heather is tougher than she looks.

"No, we're going in!" she responded firmly, pulling into Beth's driveway.

All through the welcoming breakfast, conversations, and celebrations, I was extremely reserved like a shy little boy. The opposite, in fact, of my personality both in prison and before it. Thankfully, I quickly got over that in the coming days.

Once we left Beth's, our next stop was the house we'd rented after leaving John's home, lovingly looked after in our absence by my niece and her husband. Climbing out of the passenger side of the Datsun, I looked around and said quietly, "Thank you, Lord!"

Lifting Niv Jr. out of his car seat, we walked the familiar pathway past the rose tree on the left and up to the front door. We laid Niv down. Then I brought the bags in while Heather put the kettle on for tea. While it heated, we just flopped on the couch, looked at each other, and smiled.

Ahh, home!

29

Finding a New Normal

While the freedom felt fantastic for both Heather and me, being released from prison was just the next stage of my journey back to civilisation. Now I needed to get a job and keep it, pay bills, develop a savings plan, and basically start doing normal life again.

Heather and I yearned for a break together, just us and our new son. During visits in Dhurringile, we'd made plans to go to Bateman's Bay, a coastal town popular for its snorkelling, beautiful reefs, and wildlife. But that dream was dashed by the reality of no funds. Instead, we had a much-needed catch-up with family, after which I immediately began pursuing a job. The biggest obstacle was that there was a recession going on with many companies going broke and people already out of work.

The other issue was that I had to attend parole twice a week, so any job I got had to fit around that obligation. It also meant Heather had to drive me each way as I still had no driver's licence. In fact, I didn't reacquire my licence for almost four years after getting out of prison. I couldn't count the hours Heather spent driving me places and picking me up. I consider myself very lucky to be still married! There are few women who would have put up with all that so lovingly and graciously.

Thankfully, one of the very mates I'd been drinking with on the day of my collision got me a job at a well-known national sign company, which despite the recession was hiring as they'd recently landed a major national contract.

My initial role was screwing delicate panels to aluminium frames, which would eventually be despatched in crates on trucks Australia-wide. The factory was noisy with the constant pounding of metal workers banging their hammers on steel and aluminium, the complete opposite of what I'd been living, both in prison and the prior years at the garden supply. I wondered how long I could work there while at the same time feeling guilty for thinking that way. Here I was fresh out of prison, dead-broke in a recession, fortunate to have a job but already thinking negatively!

Production sped up to the point that we were working twelve hours a day seven days a week at one stage. Tongue-in-cheek, our supervisor told us to bring in a photo of our family because we wouldn't be seeing them for a while. With no driver's licence, I was grateful to my mates for helping me with the long haul of getting back on my feet. They would pick me up from home around 5:30 a.m. and drop me off at night around 8:00 p.m. on their way home. I didn't want to neglect my spiritual life in all this, so I'd get up in time to shower and get ready, then read my Bible and pray for a short time before they picked me up.

These fifteen to sixteen-hour days became one more journey of loneliness for Heather. She'd already endured ten months of being on her own, moving to a strange town, seeing me only two days each week, going through pregnancy and raising a child for four months without a husband. Now I was asking her to basically continue that lifestyle. Her dreams of a nice family life together such as we'd planned during all her visits and phone calls appeared dashed against the wall.

At one point, Heather told me, "You might as well be back in jail considering the amount of time I see you now."

I felt caught in a way of life I couldn't control. But I still had the confidence it would all turn out fine in the end. We just needed to hang on for the ride and get through the long hours, emotional droughts, and financial problems.

The sign company had a saying written on the lunchroom wall: "You bring the attitude; we'll teach you the skills." It made a huge impression on me as the reality is that countless former inmates don't have the ability to overcome the challenges of a busy workplace where they may be sworn at, belittled, or roughly pushed to work faster and harder. They get upset, have an argument with their boss, and then leave, their pride bigger than their need for a job and income.

I've now mentored various ex-inmates and watched them get jobs, only to see some lose or leave them for one reason or another. In most circumstances after prison release, inmates find only two signposts pointing in opposite directions. One signpost reads: "NEED THIS WAY." The other reads:

"PRIDE THIS WAY." Need versus pride is what many decisions come down to in life. It's important to ditch the pride as it is a false meter of reality.

Many prisoners of war learned to swallow their pride out of desperation. They would eat anything that lived and moved and sometimes didn't move just to remain alive on this earth. That type of clear, long-term determination should override an ex-inmate's instinctive negative reaction. In too many cases, they've trained themselves to look no further into their future than next week. Need must not only overcome pride but also rejection.

Many times in those first few months, I felt like leaving. But I was continually challenged by the need to rebuild my life. I was so desperate that at one weak moment I spoke to a training company that was advertising a job lasting only five weeks. Thankfully, I didn't take it.

I ended up working there for nearly three years until their national contract was near completion. I even got Neville a job there after he got out. The old angry Neville would have lasted only a week here, but the changed Neville worked there for around eight months. Praise God for the difference He can make in a life!

As the national rollout began winding down, I wondered what I'd do next as I had no other work prospects. At one stage, I was down to three days per week and had a part-time job in the exhibition and event industry. We would set up all the stalls and displays for an expo at places like the Melbourne

Exhibition Centre, then go back a few days or nights later to dismantle it all.

Since expos typically ended in the evening, starting time for tear-down could be 11:00 p.m., finishing at 5.00 a.m. As I didn't have a driver's licence and some places weren't near public transport, Heather drove me to the various sites, then picked me up a few hours later. I was constantly embarrassed that my wife had to drive me and pick me up. The only upside besides the pay was that there was little traffic at those times. If I hadn't been married to an incredible wife like Heather, who knows where I'd be now!

Around this time, the sign company asked if I would set up a consumables store. They spent hundreds of thousands of dollars on nuts, bolts, washers, and incidental materials and had lost control over those expenditures during the rush to carry out their national contract. I set up the new store which saved them a lot of money. The company was happy enough about this that they didn't want to lose me through a lack of work. When one of the regular purchasing officers went on maternity leave, they offered me the job until she returned. That allowed me to give up my second job in the event industry. Heather was ecstatic about that!

When the purchasing officer returned from maternity leave, I was sent out to the shop floor to help where needed. I didn't care what I did so long as I got paid. When the same officer took time off for her second maternity leave, I was offered a permanent position, which I took.

Sometime in all of this, Heather and I had moved back

to Sydenham. I'd acquired a lot on the block where Mum, my sister Beth, and other family members lived. In fact, next to Mum's home right on the corner with my sister Beth's cottage on the other side. Heather and I built a house there, where we still live to this day. Being close to family and having Niv Jr. growing up next door to his grandmother was another blessing.

After those first five years of work, I was asked to take control of the sign company's transport department, as costs had skyrocketed. I did that for a further five-year stint and came in under budget, putting reliable and cost-effective transport systems into place Australia-wide.

During this period, the group general manager asked if I'd like to join the safety committee. I was voted in as chairman and safety officer. Over the next four years, building on others' work, we managed to achieve some great results, aiming for Australian Standards accreditation. Safety regulator inspectors became allies rather than enemies as we developed a leading reputation in the signage industry for workplace safety.

After that second five-year stint, I resigned from the sign company to commence working for myself as a safety consultant while also attending night school for the next four years. This is the job I do today, and I love it! It's a far cry from my unlawful behaviour on June 5th, 1990.

When I left the sign company, the group general manager wrote me a reference, calling me "an asset at the highest level, and will remain a friend of the business." I couldn't have asked for a more generous testimonial.

It's important to me that readers of this book understand that my success out of jail had very little to do with me. I didn't work as an island but with fantastic teams. The main thing, though, was that I tried to put God first in everything I did. Because of that, He blessed me with success. Some of the things God asked me to do were difficult, tiring, and put pressure on our marriage. But I knew if I obeyed Him even when it was difficult, the end result would be a blessing to me and my family.

Today, Heather, Niv Jr., and I live a great simple life. That doesn't mean we don't go through difficulties because we do. But we share a confidence that, no matter what we go through, God will walk beside us with encouragement and assurance and we'll make it through to the other side. Niv Jr. is now in his late twenties. Praise God, he has developed his own walk with God. Indeed, we are truly blessed!

30

Prison Ministry

After my release from prison, I was still passionate about helping inmates and ex-inmates, so I attended a Prison Fellowship orientation day for upcoming volunteers. While there, the current state director for Prison Fellowship Reg Worthy gave me some very sound advice. "Son, you go home and be a father and a husband. If that burning passion is still there in twelve months, come and see me then."

I followed his advice, and you know what? When the twelve months had passed, the passion wasn't there. It didn't return for some years. That advice was the best I could have received for that stage in my life. It helped my wife and I rebuild our life together and create solid foundations for the future. Instead of visiting prisons or other volunteer duties, I went home at night and weekends. I shared my time with my wife and son instead of an abundance of other people, allowing us to grow together as a family should.

Some years later, I went to another orientation day. This time I joined Prison Fellowship. I began teaching the character-training section of their courses in two of Victoria's maximum-security prisons, Barwon Prison and Port Phillip

Prison. About fifteen inmates were selected to attend these sessions. The character portion showed them the negative character traits that let them down and how they could build themselves up with positive traits. It was a rewarding experience watching these guys come to the realisation that they didn't need to be caught in the relentless cycle of prison recidivism.

Sometime later, I was also invited to join Victoria's state council for Prison Fellowship, on which I served for a number of years. It was during this time that a partnership was established between Prison Fellowship and two church denominations, Baptist and Church of Christ, to develop a special church program for ex-inmates who are on a faith journey.

We called the program Friends of Dismas (FoD). In many church traditions, Dismas is the name by which the repentant thief on the cross next to Jesus was known. We asked Kevin Maddock, a pastor well-known in prison circles, to head up the new church program. He in turn contacted Friends of Dismas in Toronto, Canada, an organisation working with ex-inmates, and asked if we could use the name in Australia. They were pleased to give us their approval.

I am the inaugural chair of the management committee. We held our grand opening fittingly in a section of the old Melbourne Jail with Pastor Tim Costello, former CEO of World Vision Australia as our keynote speaker. Tim is also our patron.

FoD proved to be a great place for ex-inmates to share and

grow in faith in a friendly and understanding environment. FoD's name soon spread through the prisons, and both men and women on their faith journey made their way to the meetings. We held them in the heart of Melbourne to make it accessible to public transport. FoD has now expanded with regular meetings also being held in Geelong and Box Hill, Victoria.

After some time, ill health forced me to relinquish my roles on both the Prison Fellowship state council and Friends of Dismas, though I remain involved in an arms-length capacity. An old kidney issue returned, resulting in me being on a dialysis machine for nine hours each night until I obtained a kidney transplant.

Currently, I mentor some inmates, ex-inmates, and others and share my testimony at various churches and other groups and networks. I am also secretary of Men's Support Mission in Williamstown, Victoria, a terrific group dedicated to helping men through life. In many circles, I find my prison experience invaluable in reaching and helping people.

Prison creates a lonely place within some people, so there can be a distancing from society after a long sentence. Some ex-inmates enter a psychological prison after they get out, and despite the number of supports or people in their lives following release, they still feel disconnected. Remixing with society is problematic for some as the remoteness, isolation, and their own lack of confidence creates an avoidance of typical responsibilities.

Take Eddie. for instance, an ex-inmate I picked up from

prison upon his release. Eddie is Aboriginal, removed from his mum early in life and allocated to foster parents. That didn't entirely work out, and he ended up spending time in juvenile detention. This progressed to prison sentences, the last of which was fifteen years.

By the time he was released, things had changed greatly in the outside world. Eddie not only battled emotional and psychological issues from being institutionalised but was met head-on with modern technological and social barriers. His first week out was so overwhelming that he spent three days lying on his bed, crying that he just wanted to go back to prison.

Among the changes was banking, which now used online and ATM services. Instead of walking up to a bank teller to deposit or withdraw his money, Eddie had to deal with bank cards and ATMs and passwords. He'd get embarrassed and angry when he put in the wrong numbers at the ATM or pressed the wrong buttons while under pressure, as he didn't want to hold up the queue behind him. Nor were people eager to offer help to a six-feet-tall, 140 kilos, extremely angry man with jail tattoos.

Public transport had also changed. Eddie had always paid cash for a tram or train ticket. Now all his usual modes of transport used a specific card that required money to be in the account. He didn't have a car licence, but now he feared taking public transport because he just didn't feel "smart" enough for the smartcard ticketing system.

Eddie also had to learn to use a mobile phone and keep it

on him everywhere he went because his parole officer might ring at any time. He kept leaving it in his room or forgetting to charge it up or turn it on, which got him into trouble with parole. He lost three phones in the first few months because he was on heavy pain medication and unaccustomed to carrying a phone.

Then there were the social issues. Before Eddie could be released, the authorities required him to have a place to live. The only place available was a boarding house in Hawthorn East. Although grateful for the lodging, the room was small, the hallway carpet smelled of stale urine, and some of the tenants would smear faeces on the toilet walls. Eddie himself was spotlessly clean and kept his room neat, but he was ashamed to invite people over.

One day, I picked Eddie up to go for a drive. We stopped at a red light, where he got out to remove his pullover as it was difficult to do in the car. The driver behind us was idly watching, not meaning any harm, when Eddie yelled at him, "What are you f*** looking at?"

When Eddie got back into the car, he defended his reaction. "Well, he was looking at me!"

"He had nowhere else to look," I commented. "You got out of the car, and his eyes simply followed you. That will happen all the time out here, so it's something you'll need to get used to."

The first time Eddie went to church after his release, he stopped outside, trying to force himself to enter. What if the church people rejected him or judged him? He finally turned around and went home, then condemned himself all week for not having the guts to go in. Desperate for a church he could call home, he worked hard on himself over the next seven days and forced himself to take the journey again. This time he entered and sat in the rear pew.

He was welcomed, but there'd been another change while Eddie was in prison. Ex-inmates like Eddie couldn't just go to church like the rest of us. The law now required notifying the church as to why he'd been in prison. Corrections Victoria also needed to be notified as well as the police. In the end, it was such a big deal that the church had to form a committee, which I was invited to attend, just so they could allow him to worship in their services. Thankfully, that church was a great example of Christ's love and persisted to overcome the new regulations.

The social problems didn't end there. When he'd entered prison the last time, Eddie had been a fit younger man. Now he was middle-aged, overweight, and due to an injury in prison, partly incapacitated. He was also paranoid and didn't know how to act socially. He'd spent most of his prison sentence in maximum security where you could be challenged for looking at someone. When he pushed an issue out here, it quickly escalated as he was still full of jail talk and aggression.

Eddie is sadly typical of some of the ex-inmates I've worked with and tried to help over the years. Many people find it hard to run from their past. History seems to have a way of dragging itself up beside us every now and then, reminding us of times and places where we've faltered.

Add a prison sentence to that—or a few in Eddie's case—where a person has been stripped of voting rights, dignity, freedom, often family and friends, and given a prisoner number now stamped on him for life, and the ex-inmate has much more to hide than the average person. Eddie had returned to a crowded society, but found he was still in a prison of perpetual loneliness. It is because there are so many Eddies out there that I believe so strongly in ministries like Prison Fellowship and Friends of Dismas.

31

Forgiveness Heals

As I mentioned at the beginning, my brother's ex-wife had made an open profession of being a born-again Christian before cheating on my brother with her police colleague. After turning on us following John's death, she'd added insult to injury by moving back into my brother's house with her partner in adultery. For approximately fifteen years, she and her common-law "husband" lived just two doors up the street from us. I will give him credit that he remained with her until her death, though I don't know if they ever officially married or whether he became a Christian.

This meant we also had to see them driving the garden supplies vehicles of the business she'd stolen from us past our house on a daily basis. To me, the decent thing once they'd taken everything would have been to move away from the family she'd wronged. But they didn't see the need or just didn't care how staying there hurt John's family.

Despite all that, Heather and I had prayed for my ex-sister-in-law from the day she'd turned on us. I don't want to sound too holier-than-thou, but all through our troubles we kept praying for her return to God. Every human being dies, but when we die, we would want to die with our Lord and Saviour Jesus Christ, not without Him, as otherwise all we have to look forward to is hell.

After many years of praying, Heather and I were browsing one day in a local Christian bookstore where we often shopped. When finished, we walked up to the counter with our purchases. As a frequent shopper, I was in the store's computerized customer base, so I gave the sales clerk my surname and the Melbourne suburb of Sydenham where we currently lived.

The sales clerk typed in the info, then asked, "Which Neyland are you?"

I was startled at the question as I knew no other Neyland who would be shopping at this Christian bookstore. I asked the clerk to turn the computer screen toward me so I could point out the right entry. Giving my address would have been easier, but I was keen to see who the other Neyland might be. My "con" worked. Ignoring privacy regulations, the clerk turned the screen so I could see. There among the entries under the surname of Neyland was both my first name, Niven, and the name of my brother's ex-wife.

I pointed calmly to my name. "This is me here."

I paid for our purchases, and we left the store. As we got into our car, Heather and I paused to give thanks to God that John's ex-wife seemed to have returned to the fold as far as her faith was concerned—or at least enough to be shopping in a Christian bookstore.

One reason for her return may have been that she'd

developed cancer. My sister Beth, who lived between our house on the corner and John's house where his ex-wife and partner now lived, had a stray cat problem. She made plans to call a cat-catcher. But residential regulations required she notify her neighbours, especially those who owned cats, to give them a heads-up before bringing in the cat-catcher. Since our former sister-in-law owned cats, Beth decided to visit her first. When John's ex-wife opened the door, Beth asked her politely how she was doing.

"Not good," our former sister-in-law responded. "I have cancer."

She invited Beth in for a cup of tea. The visit was reasonably productive as they spoke about salvation among other topics. After a few weeks, Beth noticed that John's ex-wife had a broken pipe on the outside of her house that was leaking a lot of water. When she stopped by to let our former sister-in-law know, John's ex-wife told her she'd given up fighting the cancer.

Around this time, I'd been researching cancer treatments for a friend of mine. One sounded hopeful, so when I learned that John's ex-wife had cancer, I decided to share the information with her in the hope of saving her life. Initially, I left a note in her letterbox but then decided to follow up on the note in person. I knocked on the familiar front door. After a short wait, she opened it. This was the first time we'd spoken since she called me a thief and forced me out of the business.

I explained why I was there. "I don't know if you received

the note I left in your letterbox. I just thought I'd come up and explain further in case it wasn't clear."

"I did receive it. Thank you." She invited me in for a cup of tea. I declined the cup of tea but stepped in for a brief chat. The inside of John's house had changed little in decor and even furniture since Heather and I had lived there. John's ex-wife and I exchanged some small talk. She seemed resigned to death, but there was a peace about her, and from Beth's discussion with her, I felt assured she had indeed been restored to a relationship with God, so I didn't need to worry about her eternal destiny.

That said, it was an awkward visit, especially being back in that house after all these years. Nor did she make any attempt at apology for all she'd put Heather and me through. I stayed only a short time, then wished her all the best and left. She passed away just a few months later. Her funeral was held in a church I was told she'd been attending.

Friends who knew what she'd done to our family were more sceptical of her return to Christian faith, commenting, "If it was a real repentance, she should apologise to you personally as well as to God."

Though I appreciated their expressions of support, my response was simple. "She doesn't need to make peace with me before she dies but with God, and so long as she's done that, I'm satisfied and thankful she will be spending her eternity in heaven."

For Heather and me, forgiveness was the key to having peace in our own hearts. To be able to pray for her without guile, we had to let go of all the negative stuff in the past. More importantly, we also had to let go of future financial losses that certainly came. That doesn't mean we didn't try to challenge her mischief legally.

Nothing worked in the end. But when ill-feelings rose towards her, Heather and I would both just turn them over to God. We felt it better to suffer loss than live a life filled with the poison of revenge and hatred that permeates your heart like some odourless poisonous gas. In the end, our only losses were things that pertained to this life not the next and which could either be replaced or forgotten about. As a trade-off, we found a storehouse of richness and peace in forgiveness.

Forgiveness is one of the most healing choices we can make. Thankfully, I grew up in a forgiving family where we were taught not to hold grudges. The bottom line, we all experience disappointment, whether at ourselves or others. When we disappoint ourselves, we too often head for the bottle, drugs, self-harm, negative talk or some sort of violence. Prisons are filled with people who have acted out of self-disappointment, self-loathing, and self-rejection.

The same can be said when others disappoint us. We need to forgive people when we feel they've let us down. Otherwise we spend our lives judging others and thinking we're better than them, which is unhealthy and untrue. Part of that forgiveness is recognising how many times we ourselves have disappointed others. We all need someone else's forgiveness at some time. If we want others to forgive us, we need to be willing to forgive those who disappoint us.

More than that, if we are followers of Jesus Christ, we need to forgive others because we ourselves have been forgiven of so much. Above all, God has forgiven our own sins that would have condemned us to hell without Christ's sacrifice on the cross. So if we ask just how much we should forgive those who disappoint us, that is the bar. Few of us would be able to say we've disappointed God less than others have disappointed us, so if God has forgiven us, that is the measure by which we need to forgive others, as Scripture states so clearly.

> Be kind and compassionate to one another, forgiving each other, just as God in Christ forgave you. (Ephesians 4:32)
>
> Bear with each other and forgive one another if any of you has a grievance against someone. Forgive as the Lord forgave you. (Colossians 3:13)
>
> Then Peter came to Jesus and asked, "Lord, how many times shall I forgive my brother or sister who sins against me? Up to seven times?" Jesus answered, "I tell you, not seven times, but seventy times seven." (Matthew 18:21-22)
>
> And when you stand praying, if you hold anything against anyone, forgive them, so that your Father in heaven may forgive you your sins. (Mark 11:25)

When I harbour pain and disappointment, I become the centre of my own world. I am focusing on my emotional injury and the wrong someone else has done to me. This can lead me down a path to a long-term problem where I become unpredictable and quite toxic to be around. I may appear successful and carefree, but as soon as someone rattles my cage and offends me, I get blind-sided and react to it, whether in the form of disappointment, resentment, anger, or all three.

To release those feelings and take charge of myself, I have to go further than just forgiving one person who has offended me. I need the spirit of forgiveness. This enables me to forgive every person who offends me, not just one or two people. It frees me from bottling up troubles and hating people or blowing up in anger.

We can free ourselves from a lot of pain and disappointment by learning to forgive other people as well as by seeking forgiveness from others when we ourselves have done wrong. But simply saying we will forgive is a lot easier than actually forgiving. How do we foster that spirit of forgiveness so that our hearts and minds can be released from the bondage of not forgiving? In His Sermon on the Mount, Jesus gives us the key.

> But I say to you, love your enemies, bless them that curse you, do good to them that hate you, and pray for them who despitefully use you, and persecute you. (Matthew 5:44)

This isn't some fairy-tale magic trick but a very real way of dealing with people who push our buttons. By following these suggestions, we free ourselves from the prison of those negative feelings. They don't hold power over us anymore. You may feel that is unrealistic. Yet, loving isn't an emotion, it's an act of your will. You can start by praying for those who've hurt you and by deliberately doing good things for them. As you do so, you'll be amazed how God gives you actual love for those people.

When we forgive, we have no idea how far that little action will reach. It teaches our children the right way to deal with conflict. When we don't forgive, we are not the only one being poisoned. We pass unforgiveness onto our kids, and they grow up with that same poisonous spirit.

But the purpose of forgiveness isn't just to heal ourselves. It is also to heal the person being forgiven. When we ask God to give us the spirit of forgiveness, we start to see others the way Jesus sees them, the way He sees us, as fallen individuals needing help. That in turn can lead to making peace with the other person as Heather and I were able to do. Even if the other person never admits fault or asks forgiveness, they may at least make peace with God and others.

Restorative justice programs or meetings, where victims and offenders come face to face to tell their side of the story and express their feelings, have been useful tools for this type of healing. Figuring out why someone has done something wrong to us, whether real or an injury we believe they've done, goes a long way to understanding the full picture, not just our position in it. It helps us rise above our own personal opinions and pain. The ultimate goal is to bring peace between the two parties, just as Christ's forgiveness of our own sins brought us peace and reconciliation with God and with those we once thought of as enemies.

> For He [Christ] Himself is our peace, who has made the two groups [Jews and Gentiles] one and has destroyed the barrier,

the dividing wall of hostility . . . His purpose was to create in Himself one new humanity out of the two, thus making peace, and in one body to reconcile both of them to God through the cross. (Ephesians 2:14-16)

For God was pleased . . . through Him [Christ] to reconcile to Himself all things, whether things on earth or things in heaven, by making peace through His blood, shed on the cross. (Colossian 1:19-20)

32

Epilogue: Final Reflections

If you have read this entire book to this point, you now know just how amazing the grace of our Lord Jesus Christ has been throughout my journey to prison and back. In Scripture, we are told that our lifespan is limited.

> Our days may come to seventy years, or eighty if our strength endures, yet the best of them are but trouble and sorrow, for they quickly pass, and we fly away . . . Teach us to number our days, that we may gain a heart of wisdom. (Psalm 90:10, 12)

In other words, seventy years is the average human lifespan, maybe an extra decade or so if we enjoy exceptionally good health. That isn't long. If we are to do anything positive with our lives, we need to understand how short life is and seek God's wisdom so we may live the years God gives us to His glory.

I was exactly halfway through my allotted seventy years right to the very day—my thirty-fifth birthday—when my decision to drive unlawfully set in motion a chain of events that would haunt the rest of my life, costing me my brother, business, savings and other financial assets, even friends.

When we do stupid stuff, we rarely realise how many people we affect. In my case, I don't mean the people I directly affected by the collision but people who had faith in me. And by that, I mean a *lot* of faith along with accompanying expectations and accountabilities.

I was privileged to be born into a devoutly Christian home, and the Bible tells us that to whom much is given, much will be required (Luke 12:48). No particular pressure was placed on me, but Christian parents have hopes and a vision for their children, and there were expectations such as I now have for my own son. And we should have expectations as Christian parents, as we do not put our heart and soul into raising children to see them wander off into a lost eternity.

My parents were no different, yearning to see the fruits of their godly labour in their children's lives. But I chose to spend much of my time in a state of rebellion and lawlessness, not as a wild criminal but as someone confident of where he was eventually bound but who in the meantime enjoyed crossing over the line from time to time. I was rather like the biblical Jonah who wasn't willing to fulfil the task to which God had called him, running instead full-speed in the opposite direction until God had enough and engineered a monumental crossroad he could never have dreamed of in all his years.

In Jonah's case, that involved being swallowed by a whale-sized fish (Jonah 1-2). In mine, it involved being swallowed up by a huge, impersonal prison system. For both of us, it took some unpleasant experiences and sincere repentance before God felt we were ready for release and a return to His service.

After the collision, my mother told me that it had taken place just about the exact time of day I was born thirty-five years earlier. I took that as a serious warning from God. I'd played around with God for my first thirty-five years, sometimes being sincere in my faith but other times disobedient and frivolous. Now it was half-time, and like Jonah, I'd reached a catastrophic crossroad. God was telling me to stop my foolishness and get real!

I am so thankful my faithful God and heavenly Father was there from the beginning, even in the car when I was upside-down trying to come to terms with what had just happened and making some fast decisions. He was there with me leading up to the court date. He was with me all the way through prison. And He is present in our lives now.

Toward the end of my sentence, one Dhurringile inmate, a bank robber who wasn't particularly fond of Christians, told me, "Niven, I fear when you leave, this prison will go back to the way it was."

I am no saint or hero of the faith. Nor am I particularly bold in the Lord, just sociable and sometimes loud. But God was definitely working in Dhurringile, and it was obvious even to those who weren't interested in knowing Him. During my short sentence there, I suppose a lot of Christian ministry did happen, though I didn't really do any of it with much forward planning.

What I did do was try to surrender myself daily to God

as best I could and let God have His sovereign way with me without my interference or fear. As I did this, things got done, and relationships grew. I didn't care if those I helped were inmates, prison officers, or even the prison itself. Neither did I care what the inmates were in for. I believed God was calling me to recognise that different people were on different pathways and places in their lives and needed understanding before judgment—or instead of it.

So strong was my commitment to that strange sort of ministry, I distinctly recall saying to my wife as we approached the last day of my sentence, "I really shouldn't be leaving here. I have too much work still to do."

God was doing a great work in that prison, and I felt like I was running out on people who would be left still fighting their spiritual battles. But as King Solomon, the wisest man in history, stated:

> There is a time for everything, and a season for every activity under the heavens (Ecclesiastes 3:1)

That chapter goes on to list how different things like planting, building, speaking, even loving have a time to start and a time to finish. My season of ministry at Dhurringile had ended with the completion of my prison sentence. God in His sovereignty would raise up new people, whether inmates like Trevor, Darryl, and Stretch or volunteers like Ted and Dallas, to carry on His work. But despite the reminder of that scripture, it was still quite gut-wrenching to leave these people behind. I had to remind myself that they were in God's hands, not mine.

Had I not gone to prison, I would likely have spent the last thirty years building a successful business and living for myself with God coming second, just as I had so many times in the past. My sentence put a stop to that. I was taken to a dark place where God Himself was my light, and the course of my life changed. Heather and I were blessed beyond measure during my prison sentence and continued to be blessed after it. This includes receiving money in our letterbox when we were in deep need from total strangers, many still unknown to us today, as well as people we knew. We experienced pure-hearted, unadulterated, guileless Christian generosity.

We also received wise counsel from our pastor, who even under extreme pressures of life himself knew just what to write in a letter or say on visits to keep our heads up and focussed on the future. He once wrote me:

> I guess you're learning the discipline of prison life. I hope you will be able to tell others of this way of life, the way someone else dictates every part of every day. So it is with our life in Christ. We must learn to be willing prisoners. You will be able to relate this experience to the rest of the church. Think on this, add some meat, and send some thoughts onto others. We are in the middle of troubled times.

I wasn't in prison a long time as sentences go, and Heather and I are both grateful for that. But it was long enough for God to deal with me in the way He wanted. In prison, He had my undivided attention, which is challenging in this busy world to get from any of us. I wasn't only away from the crowded city and those I loved but also away from all forms of distraction so God could walk me through my sentence getting the things done that He wished and growing me into the man He wanted me to be. Those who know me realise I still have a long way to go, but God is faithful and, above all, patient with me.

Of course, it would have been better if God hadn't needed to put me in prison to get my full attention. It is always better and certainly a lot less painful to give yourselves in obedience to God without the force of a "Jonah's whale" being needed. In truth, I wasn't a mature adult before my collision and prison. I drank to excess, was only half-committed to the Lord, and had PLOM's Disease. These are very restrictive barriers to a healthy relationship with Jesus Christ, let alone to ever becoming mature. My changes for the better are due to my prison sentence. Let's make no mistake. I needed the "time out" I was given! Make sure you don't.

Have I felt guilt over the years for dragging Heather through all this? You'd better believe it. Heather was an innocent, loving wife who through no fault of her own (except falling for me, poor girl!) endured far more than she'd ever expected when she accepted my marriage proposal. Before we were married, we'd been looking at house plans, talking of where we'd live, how many kids we'd have, and growing old together with a little cottage garden and grandkids running around.

That's a far cry from the traumatic, penniless existence I gave her for the first few years of marriage. But God also used Heather to achieve His purposes. She has a loving, cheerful disposition and makes people feel better for having talked with her. She was a real comfort to wives and girlfriends of inmates and their kids. Since they knew she was in a similar situation driving an old car back and forth from prison with little money and a baby on the way, they could relate to her. The difference was that she confidently trusted in her Saviour, and this was a shining testimony to others there who really needed it.

Life didn't turn out the way Heather and I thought it would when we got engaged. God didn't set me free from the courtroom with an easier penalty. Neither did I get my business back, regardless of my hopes. Instead, He gave me what I needed. If Heather and I had married while I was still living my former life, I have no doubt at all we'd have divorced within a few years. That collision saved our marriage as well!

As we come to the end of our time together in the pages of this book, it is my deep hope and prayer for each of you reading that your life will be impacted by the grace of God as mine and Heather's was during my prison sentence. We were blessed by that unmerited, undeserved favour of our gracious Saviour, who saw both of us through every day of my sentence and guided us through every step of that difficult season of re-entering society.

What is your life like? What do you seek? More money,

a new car, another house, less pressure, more holidays, a greater financial portfolio? Does God enter your thoughts? Are you a one day per week Christian? Not a Christian at all? We don't know when this life ends. Whether a full seventy- or eighty-year lifespan or only one more day due to an unexpected catastrophe, the Bible tells us that our time here on earth is short and fleeting.

> Show me, Lord, my life's end and the number of my days; let me know how fleeting my life is. You have made my days a mere handbreadth; the span of my years is as nothing before you. Everyone is but a breath, even those who seem secure. (Psalm 39:4-5)
>
> Now listen, you who say, "Today or tomorrow we will go to this or that city, spend a year there, carry on business and make money." Why, you do not even know what will happen tomorrow. What is your life? You are a mist that appears for a little while and then vanishes. (James 4:13-14)

If you'd asked anybody who knew me and John as to who would probably die first, the answer every time would have been me. When John the Baptist and Jesus both began preaching, they cried out, "Repent: for the kingdom of heaven is at hand" (Matthew 3:2; 4:17). I never quite understood what that meant until that out-of-the-blue collision where my life continued while John's abruptly ended. One second, he was here. The next, he'd entered the following world. The kingdom of heaven was at hand for him. It was immediate.

I am so thankful to God that John was assured of his faith in

Jesus Christ and is now in a far better place. But many won't be when their own time is at hand. Do you know where you will be going when you die?

Jesus Christ calls those who want to be His disciples to do far more than simply call themselves Christians. We must be willing to give up our own desires, ambitions, wealth, fame, and all else this world offers in exchange for what actually has value in eternity—our soul, our relationship with God, our loved-ones who know God, eternal life in heaven.

> Then He [Jesus] said to them all, "If anyone desires to come after Me, let him deny himself, and take up his cross daily, and follow Me. For whoever desires to save his life will lose it, but whoever loses his life for My sake will save it. For what profit is it to a man if he gains the whole world, and is himself destroyed or lost? (Luke 9:23-25)

Denying ourselves seems counter-productive, but the riches we get following our Saviour are far greater both in this life and the next. Jesus also calls us not to work for all those things which perish with this life but to put our time into activities that will go with us to heaven (Matthew 6:19-21). This includes people who come into God's Kingdom because of our witness. Those are the real riches!

I pray that this book will challenge you to put your life at the disposal of your Lord and Saviour. Not just on your church day or other religious events, but by giving Him your whole life. And may I just finish by praying this scriptural benediction over you, which says far better than I what my hope and prayer is for you as you move forward through the remaining years God has appointed to you on this earth.

Now may the God of peace who brought up our Lord Jesus from the dead, that great Shepherd of the sheep, through the blood of the everlasting covenant, make you complete in every good work to do His will, working in you what is well pleasing in His sight, through Jesus Christ, to whom be glory forever and ever. Amen. (Hebrews 13:20-21)

Appendix 1: Helps For Getting Through Life and Prison

As I look back over those ten months in prison, I can pinpoint many things I did that helped me get through my sentence. Here are the top ten that helped me and I trust will help you too.

- **I tried to give my future to the Lord,** whatever that was. This included not trying to engineer or scheme one step of it. I had to abandon my future in my mind and not plan ahead. That way God could lead, and hopefully I would follow.

- **I tried to be myself.** God can't deal with us if we're hoping and trying to be someone else. Sometimes it's hard being ourselves, particularly when we don't like what we see. But God made us a particular way, and He can and will use anything for His purpose, even us.

- **I got rid of judgments and biases.** There are codes in prison and biases inmates develop, such as not mixing with paedophiles, or ex-coppers. But as far as I was concerned, we were all criminals, and the outside world has a distaste for most of our crimes, not just a few. God will take anyone who repents, so I had to keep an open heart for everybody.

- **I spent a lot of time with God.** This meant I'd be praying and talking to God most of the day, often under my breath. This deepened my relationship with God and made us friends.

- **I made quick requests to God** to help me make decisions. If in a problematic situation, I'd pray a simple prayer quickly in my mind: *Lord, please help me here!* No one else would know, but I needed God's wisdom a lot in there, and He always answered.

- **I studied my Bible and prayed a lot.** I'd always loved praying and reading the Bible, but while inside I put the pedal-to-the-metal and developed routines to accomplish more of it. If I neglected my reading and prayer, days went bad for me every time and my emotions dragged me wherever they wanted like a doll dragged through the mud by an uncaring child.

- **I rose early most mornings to get things done.** Once in my own unit, I was up around 5:00 a.m. every morning to study and pray, other than a couple of times when I had the flu and a couple of other brief intervals when I allowed depression to enter my mind.

- **I saw it all as the Lord's work.** I tried to keep selfishness out of my daily routines, especially when it came to giving my time and effort freely to Christian ministry and counselling. Selfishness is the enemy of God.

- **I spent time with people.** I like people, so that may be easier for me than some others. Most of my prison time was spent with people from many different walks of life and backgrounds, some who'd gone through tragic experiences that contributed to why they ended up inside. It is important for Christians to spend time with people as they are our field of ministry. If not people, then what else is there? I don't like viewing people as "ministry" or "work" but as friends.

- **I tried to stay in God's rest.** I sought to keep my mind and heart in a state of rest despite the troubles and amount of work around me. It didn't always work. But when it did, the negative aspects of prison life had little impact.

Appendix 2: A Prayer for a Relationship with God

This prayer simply refers to the words spoken by a person to God when he or she has recognised their sin, their need for forgiveness of sin, and their need for a relationship with God through Jesus Christ. That forgiveness and relationship with God is only possible through the sacrifice for our sins on the cross and resurrection of Jesus Christ. When you confess your sins, ask God for forgiveness, believe in your heart that God has raised Christ from the dead, and profess your faith in Jesus Christ, at that very moment you are born again into God's family and have the assurance of eternal life in heaven when you die.

The following verses give some of the biblical foundation behind God's wonderful plan of salvation:

For all have sinned and fall short of the glory of God. (Romans 3:23)

For the wages of sin is death, but the gift of God is eternal life in Christ Jesus our Lord. (Romans 6:23)

> If you confess with your mouth the Lord Jesus and believe in your heart that God has raised Him from the dead, you will be saved. For with the heart one believes unto righteousness, and with the mouth confession is made unto salvation. (Romans 10:9-10)
>
> For God so loved the world that He gave His only begotten Son, that whoever believes in Him should not perish but have everlasting life. For God did not send His Son into the world to condemn the world, but that the world through Him might be saved. He who believes in Him is not condemned; but he who does not believe is condemned already, because he has not believed in the name of the only begotten Son of God. (John 3:16-18)

If you want to repent of your sins and receive Jesus Christ as Saviour right now, the following is an example of the "Sinner's Prayer" you can use. Simply read the words, speaking from your heart to God.

> Father, I know that I have broken your laws and my sins have separated me from you. I repent and am truly sorry. Now I want to turn away from my past sinful life and turn toward you. Please forgive me and help me avoid sinning again. I believe that your Son Jesus Christ died for my sins, was resurrected from the dead, is alive, and hears my prayer. I invite Jesus to become the Lord of my life to rule and reign in my heart from this day forward. Please send your Holy Spirit to help me obey You and to do Your will for the rest of my life. In Jesus's name I pray. Amen!

If you decided to repent of your sins and receive Christ today, welcome to God's family. Now, as a way to grow closer to

Him, the Bible tells us to follow up on our commitment. Here are some of the next steps you will want to begin in following Jesus Christ.

- Tell someone else about your new faith in Christ.
- Spend time with God each day. It doesn't have to be a long period of time. Just develop the daily habit of praying to God and reading His Word, the Bible. Ask God to increase your faith and your understanding of the Bible.
- Seek fellowship with other followers of Jesus. Develop a group of believing friends to answer your questions and support you.
- Find a local church where you can worship God. Be sure to ask a committed Christian to help you find a good one.
- Get baptised as commanded by Christ.

Appendix 3: Bible Personages Familiar With Prison

A surprising number of biblical personages spent time in prison, some for their own wrong-doing, others for prophesying God's Word and preaching the gospel. Here are some of the best-known if you'd like to spend some time exploring their stories.

- Joseph, one of Jacob's twelve sons who was sold into slavery in Egypt by his brothers and later saved the people from famine (Genesis 37-50).
- Samson, one of Israel's early warriors and judges, imprisoned by his enemies after disobeying God (Judges 16:21-22).
- Jeremiah, one of God's prophets imprisoned by the king for prophesying God's Word (Jeremiah 32:2; 38).
- Micaiah, another prophet imprisoned by the king for prophesying truth (1 Kings 22).
- Kings of Judah Manasseh, Jehoiachin, and Zedekiah (2

Kings 24:8-10, 27-30; 25:1-7; 2 Chronicles 33:1-20), all captured and imprisoned by enemies for evil and rebellion against God; Manasseh repented and was eventually freed.

- The prophet Daniel and his three friends, each imprisoned for their faith during their captivity in Babylon (Daniel 3, 6).
- John the Baptist, executed by King Herod while in prison. (Matthew 14:1-12; Mark 6).
- Jesus, imprisoned between His arrest and crucifixion (Matthew 26:47-27).
- The apostle Peter, jailed for preaching the gospel (Acts 12).
- Other apostles and early Christians jailed for their faith (Acts 5:17-29; 8:3).
- The apostle Paul and his ministry partner Silas, who were whipped and put in stocks (Acts 16).
- The apostle Paul imprisoned for two years in Israel for preaching the gospel (Acts 22-27).
- The apostle Paul, imprisoned in Rome for preaching the gospel and eventually executed there (Philippians 1:12-14; 2 Timothy 2:9; 4:6-18).
- Other martyrs for their faith (Hebrews 12:36).

www.ingramcontent.com/pod-product-compliance
Lightning Source LLC
Chambersburg PA
CBHW071419290426
44108CB00014B/1893